MAGNIFICENT MASQUERADE

The Strange Case of Dr. Coster and Mr. Musica

Books by the same author

The Marked Woman

Modigliani: The Body of Love

Wake Up to Tomorrow

Magnificent Masquerade

THE STRANGE CASE
OF DR. COSTER
AND MR. MUSICA

Charles Keats

ILLUSTRATED WITH PHOTOGRAPHS

FUNK & WAGNALLS COMPANY, INC.
NEW YORK

For
Candy and Alan

Preface

Ever since the hectic days of December, 1938, when I was covering the unmasking of Dr. F. Donald Coster and the resurrection of Philip Musica, I have felt that the amazing double life of this perverted genius demanded a book. I am gratified that it has finally arrived between covers and I would like to acknowledge my sincere appreciation to those who aided me in the preparation and completion of the book.

My own file of material from the Bridgeport *Sunday Herald,* for which I covered the story, the Bridgeport *Post,* the defunct Bridgeport *Times Star*—the last paper I worked on— the New York *Times,* the New York *Herald Tribune,* and the New York *Daily News* was augmented by records and memorabilia in the Bishop Room of the Bridgeport library. I particularly would like to thank June Katherine Csoltko, in charge there, for her gracious assistance. Articles in *Fortune, The New Yorker,* the *Saturday Evening Post, True,* and the *Wall Street Journal* were also helpful.

To Doris McNeil, my thanks on two counts. First, she did a meticulous job of typing my manuscript. Second, as the private secretary to Julian Thompson, McKesson & Robbins treasurer and key figure in the rise and fall of Dr. Coster, she contributed intimate details of the story.

My thanks are also extended to the many other friends, acquaintances, and former employees of the company, too numerous to list, who were on the scene at the time and who provided vital bits and pieces to the story.

—C. K.

Contents

1 : The Musicas of Mulberry Bend

THE BANK president cleared his throat and said: "Dr. Coster, we think you should be a candidate for President of the United States."

Dr. F. Donald Coster made no immediate comment. He fingered his close-cropped mustache and looked thoughtfully around at the delegation gathered in his Connecticut living room. His guests were New York financiers, staid New England bankers, attorneys, industrialists, respected politicians—influential Republicans all. It was only 1937, but the Republicans, still stunned by the Roosevelt landslide that had buried Alf Landon's sunflower the year before, knew that they had a Herculean job of digging out and that they needed an early start. They also needed an attractive candidate—and who would be a more brilliant standard-bearer than Dr. Coster, the genius who had piloted the venerable pharmaceutical firm of McKesson & Robbins through the perilous shoals of 1929 and who in the intervening years had restored its dynastic glory to a multimillion-dollar pinnacle?

"We want to assure you of our complete support," continued the spokesman, "both moral and financial. And we would like permission to use your name in our preliminary plans."

"I am flattered and honored by your proposal," said Dr. Coster. He paused, squinting owlishly through his horn-rimmed glasses at his expectant guests. He seemed to reflect for a long moment, while his eyes sought out the large portrait of Theodore Roosevelt, his idol since boyhood, which hung on the wall at his left. He knew that his New England and New York friends would find backing in other parts of the nation. In a drawer of his desk there was a telegram he had just received from California Republicans in high places, also pleading with him to declare himself. There was a ground swell in the making. It could very well carry him far —at least to the 1940 convention, if not to the White House.

"Gentlemen," said Dr. Coster, "I cannot tell you how much I appreciate your confidence in me. I wish I could find it possible to join with you in this important project. However, personal reasons, which I am sure you will understand, dictate my reluctant regrets."

The delegates understood, or thought they did. A man of Dr. Coster's stature, with multimillion-dollar interests, could scarcely be expected to give up his personal fortune to be a sacrificial lamb on the Rooseveltian altar. So in 1940 the Republicans nominated Wendell Willkie, the barefoot boy from Wall Street.

A year after the momentous Connecticut meeting, federal agents discovered the significant telegram from Coster's West Coast boosters, and, needless to say, they almost flipped. The wire still reposes as the prize exhibit in the colorful, incredible Coster file.

dominantly Irish; the Italian families were outnumbered almost ten to one. By the time Philip Musica became one of the crawling thousands of the infamous anthill, the ratio had become almost fifty-fifty, but the bosses of the underworld were still sons of Erin. When Philip was four years old, the notorious Whyo gang, which made its headquarters in Mulberry Bend, was decapitated by the hanging—for murder—of its two leaders, Danny Driscoll and Danny Lyons, in the Tombs. Other Whyos—who would kill a man for $100—included Red Rocks Farrell, Hoggy Walsh, Slops and Baboon Connolly, and Googy Corcoran.

The Musicas' neighbors—3,000 of them jammed into Baxter Street between Canal and Chatham (now Park Row)—lived at such addresses as Bandits' Roost, Thieves' Alley, Kerosene Row, and Bottle Alley. They disported themselves in such dives as The Morgue in the Bowery, Milligan's Hell, just two blocks away from Philip's birthplace on Broome Street, and Boiled Oysters Malloy's basement emporium on Centre Street near the Tombs, where whisky was three shots for a dime.

By the time Philip entered his teens, the power of the Whyos was declining. In the last years of the century, the violence of the Irish was giving way to the cunning of the Southern Italians. A band of beady-eyed men in dark clothes, the padrones, the guides who had fattened on the waves of ignorant and bewildered immigrants from the Mediterranean, had taken over the economy of Mulberry Bend. The padrone was the king of Little Italy. He ruled by persuasion if possible, by blackmail if necessary.

If a man was strong and a friend of the padrone, he could earn as much as $2 a day. For an extra $12.50 he could get United States citizenship papers. The padrone could get work for women, too; they could sew at home, finishing pants at three-and-a-half cents a pair, and by working twelve to sixteen hours a day, they could make as much as thirty-five cents. This was more than small children could make in a ten-hour day; they got only two-and-a-half cents an hour and therefore made only a quarter. But they were the lucky kids, because they knew the padrone. The unlucky ones, the twelve-year-old penny prostitutes, sold their flea-bitten bodies to grown men in backyards and hallways for a copper or two, or even a bag of stale candy on hungry days. Ten percent of the dead in Mulberry Bend were buried in Potter's Field.

Why adolescent Philip Musica did not founder in this vicious cesspool is perhaps a key to his character. The iniquity of Mulberry Bend was by no means reserved for adults. Cop-hating brats formed gangs that would make present-day juvenile delinquents look like Boy Scouts. A prodigy called Baby-face Willie dominated the Baxter Street Dudes which, though ostensibly a troupe of child minstrels, would do anything for a price. There was Italian Dave, the Fagin of Mulberry Bend, who trained a stable of forty boys in shoplifting, picking pockets, burglary, and various other subdivisions of sneak-thievery. And there were numerous independent juvenile gangs, such as the expert team of child pickpockets masterminded by Crazy Butch. Crazy Butch abandoned an honest career as a shoeshine and newsboy, begun at the age of eight, for the greener fields of purse snatching at the age of ten. When he was thirteen, Crazy Butch trained a stolen dog (which he rechristened Rabbi) to snatch handbags and muffs from careless females. In the late 1890's, Crazy Butch had two dozen beardless apprentice dips fanning out over lower Manhattan while he supervised operations on a bicycle.

At the height of his power, Butch was killed in a fight over a woman.

Although Philip Musica grew up with the stench of Mulberry Bend in his nostrils, a smell that was to linger in his subconscious as long as he lived, he managed to keep his nose above the noisome neighborhood norm. While his teen-age contemporaries were earning nickels as runners for Mulberry Bend whorehouses, Philip was exploring the higher echelons of the New World. At the age of twelve he had already found a hero image: the new president of the New York Board of Police Commissioners, a man who had once been defeated for the mayoralty of New York and had yet to achieve fame with his Rough Riders at San Juan Hill—Theodore Roosevelt. Instinctively the boy Philip sensed and admired the future president's leadership qualities. Assiduously he stored up memories of the great man, which he was to treasure the rest of his life. He haunted the police commissioner's office on Broome Street when he thought his hero was due to arrive or depart. He listened to the high-pitched Harvard voice, noted the superior kind of English that was being spoken, and made careful observations of dress and mannerisms. He was, as Broadway would put it, a quick study.

Philip Musica as a boy already felt that he was of the superior breed. He spurned the neighborhood hoodlums who would have acclaimed him boss of one of their gangs. He would have none of their petty five-and-ten-cent defiance of the law. The boy, who forty years later was to refer to the employees of his business empire as "maggots," had his eyes on bigger things, and he was willing to wait. Meanwhile he was educating himself. Formal schooling bored him. Classroom studies keyed to the slow grasp of dullards and "greenhorns" he absorbed like a sponge in a thunder shower. The boy who later would claim the degrees of Doctor of Philosophy and Doctor of Medicine from Heidelberg University quit school at the age of fourteen.

Philip did not stop learning, though. He was a voracious reader, and his retentive mind did not waste a syllable. Instead of the geography of maps, he studied the social geography of the city. With an adoring mongrel at his heels, he ventured as far west as Broadway, then as far north as Washington Square. He roved eastward to the Fulton Street ferry and reconnoitered the far reaches of Brooklyn where he was amazed to find elegant new houses, many of them for the exclusive use of a single family! This was a life to dream about. This was a life he would have for his own.

But it was not a dream for himself alone. Despite his complex and devious personality, the loner, the disdainful scorner of his peers, was completely devoted to his family. For Philip, it was more than an Italianate trait. It was a cult, a compulsion. His family was growing. Every year or so another brother or sister made a puling appearance at 377 Broome Street. After Philip came Louise, then Grace, followed in order by Arthur, George, Robert, Evelyn, and Lucy. Philip, as the first-born, accepted his share of responsibility for each new mouth to feed.

The fierce loyalty that bound the Musicas tightly together in poverty was never to waver as Philip clawed his way upward to dazzling opulence. Papa Antonio, as tradition demanded, received the title and perquisites of head of the family. Philip recognized his position; he also recognized that his father was as ineffectual as he was genial, that he was quite content to remain a barber in New York, just as he would have been happy to remain a barber in Naples. Mama Assunta Musica also recognized her husband's limitations, but she was not resigned to them.

Mama Assunta was a determined and dedicated woman. She was tiny, under five feet tall, and in her Mulberry Bend days possessed a compact figure that later, with childbearing and sumptuous living, was to expand until she was roughly spherical. It was she who groomed Philip to be the dynamo of the family. She fed his ambition, spurred his drive, and sharpened his native shrewdness. She nagged her husband into seeking means of augmenting his income to provide for his steadily augmented family. With the birth of baby Lucy, the seventh of Philip's sisters and brothers, Papa Antonio finally opened a small grocery store stocked with the cheeses, the sausages, the cured fish, and the condiments dear to the palates of his countrymen. He continued his barbering part-time, however, for his offspring had voracious appetites.

When Philip Musica quit school at fourteen, he joined his father in the store. Two years later, when he was sixteen, and the nineteenth century was in its hundredth year, Philip became operating head of the business. It was thriving, and Papa Antonio put away his razors for good.

Young Philip was an instinctive trader. Even at sixteen he had a flair for business. He was an astute merchandiser, and although he had never seen the land of his forefathers, he was unerring in his choice of Italian viands that would make his customers' mouths water. The fat mortadèllas, the slim Genoa salamis, and the pale plump provolone cheeses that hung from the ceiling in the gloom of the little shop gave off heavenly aromas. The kegs of anchovies could not be surpassed in Mulberry Bend. His Gorgonzolas were soft and golden and as beautifully green-veined as Italian marble, and his Romanos and Parmigianos were of the exact hardness for proper grating. People came from blocks around to buy Mama Assunta's homemade ravioli and fettuccine.

Much as the clink of coins on the counter of A. Musica & Son delighted the ears of Philip, much as the steadily growing income gave the family a stable, comfortable security, the routine of the store, the galling necessity of bargaining with the old ladies with black shawls around their white hair, penny-pinching vixens who sniffed at his dried mushrooms and pinched his baccalà, drove him potty. As soon as he had broken his oldest younger brother Arthur into the ABC's of storekeeping, Philip set out for the East River docks, which he had previously explored, to find a way to eliminate the profit of the middleman. If he could import direct from Italy, he could undersell his competitors and still make a bigger profit.

In a few months, Philip had mastered the essentials of the import-export business. He had not only secured agencies for well-known Italian exporters of olive oil and spices, but he also had begun to specialize in Italian cheeses. He was still in his teens when he became a full-fledged wholesaler on his own, collecting double markups, underselling other jobbers, and making A. Musica & Son one of the most prosperous retailers of Italian specialties on the Lower East Side.

In 1904, when Philip was twenty, he decided that he had it made. After consultation with Mama Assunta, he decided to put the smells, the ratty corruption, and the grinding poverty of Mulberry Bend behind him forever. He journeyed to Brooklyn and made a down payment on an impressive mansion in the fashionable Bay Ridge section that he had been eying enviously for nearly ten years.

When the Musica clan—Papa, Mama, Philip, and his seven brothers and sisters—relinquished their Broome Street tenement to the roaches and moved into an elegant home of their own, most of them thought they were dreaming. To Mama Assunta, however, it was a dream come true, a dream of twenty years' nurturing.

To Philip Musica, it was just the first step on the way up.

2 : Man About Town

PHILIP MUSICA'S success as an importer and wholesaler of Italian cheeses was phenomenal, and he enjoyed every minute of it. His firm was grossing around half a million dollars a year, and the net (there was no income tax in the early 1900's), after providing lavishly for the Musica clan, left plenty for Philip to become a dashing Broadway figure.

He dressed impeccably and expensively. He smoked only the finest Havana cigars. His diamond ring was a menace to weak, unprotected eyes. He dined at Delmonico's, Bustanoby's, Rector's, and took his coffee and brandy in Peacock Alley at the Waldorf. He was an intimate of Enrico Caruso, and when his fellow Neapolitan was singing at the Metropolitan Opera, Philip's magnificent black mustache was often seen in a grand tier box. He was a fast man with a dollar, a connoisseur of wine and women, a bon vivant who liked to think of himself as a Diamond Jim Brady with taste. For five years the world was his oyster, and he wore its pearl as a stickpin.

Suddenly, in 1909, lightning struck from his cloudless sky. The administration of Mayor G. B. McClellan was under attack. Candidate William J. Gaynor, backed by a reform movement, campaigned against McClellan by screaming "corruption." The newspapers, taking up the cry, dug up columns of scandal along the East River waterfront. In a vain attempt to stave off a Gaynor victory in November, McClellan's henchmen organized their own investigation of the docks.

Among the earliest victims of the din against sin were the Musicas. Outstanding among the *nouveaux riches* of the waterfront, they were natural targets for a sweeping inquiry. Investigators wanted to know how they had managed to come so far so fast. They soon found out.

The scandal probers got their answers by using the carrot-and-stick technique on customs inspectors. Promising the inspectors immunity and simultaneously putting them under tremendous pressure to talk, the investigators found that the secret of the phenomenal Musica success was simple indeed: bribery.

The tariff on imported cheese was calculated on the basis of weight. The Musicas had been paying bribes of up to $500 a shipment—in early-1900 dollars—to certain customs men for recording the incoming Gorgonzolas and Parmigianos at a fraction of the actual scale readings. The inquiry showed that the Musica profits ran 500 percent higher than those of their rival cheese importers who did not benefit by the same savings on tariff payments.

Mama Assunta's wonderful dream and Philip's glamorous world of bright lights and Broadway beauties collapsed together on October 29, 1909. On that date a federal grand jury indicted Antonio and Philip Musica for fraud.

On that date also Philip Musica became actual head of the clan. To save the titular head of the family from disgrace, Philip accepted full and sole responsibility for the misdeeds of A. Musica & Son. He made a deal with the federal authorities: if the charges against his father were dropped, he would enter a plea of guilty.

Somehow the deal was shunted around the U.S. attorney prosecuting the case and agreed to on a higher level. Whether Philip had already begun his career of charming important people in high places during his whirlwind courtship of Broadway, or whether Musica dollars had again successfully tickled the soft underbelly of corruption, is not clear from the record. In any event, Philip got off with a one-year sentence to the New York State Reformatory at Elmira, which was at that time receiving federal prisoners.

Stripped of his finery and shorn of his great black mustache at the age of twenty-five, Philip might easily have thought that Destiny had turned her back on him. However, a "mug shot" taken of him at the time, with the number M630-D hung across his chest, pictures him as a slightly bewildered, not in the least contrite or downhearted, young man. His close-cropped hair beginning to grow thin in front, his slightly protruding eyes, his pouting underlip and square, jutting jaw, gave him the appearance of a young Mussolini.

Immediately on his arrival at Elmira, Philip set himself apart from the rest of the inmates. He would have nothing to do with the rank-and-file prisoners. Identifying himself as an accountant, he was assigned to the administrative offices of the reformatory. Officials there noted for the record that young Musica was a prisoner of impressive intelligence and ability.

Young Musica made good use of his intelligence and ability, plus, it would seem, mysterious contacts he had made while rubbing elbows with the great and near great in recent years, to alter his status as prisoner. Details of how he accomplished his ends are as obscure today as they were then, but he did not languish long in durance vile. Five and one-half months after sentencing, Philip Musica, admitted swindler, walked out of Elmira a free man. His sentence had been commuted by William Howard Taft, President of the United States.

Whatever the channels that brought the plight of the Musica boy from Mulbery Bend to the favorable attention of the White House, they most certainly did not flow through the office of the Attorney General of the United States. The men who had tried so hard and long to convict both Musicas made their fury known when they learned of Philip's release. Henry A. Wise, the U.S. district attorney who prosecuted the case, characterized Philip as "no ordinary criminal" and protested:

> He was sentenced to one year in Elmira and I publicly declared the whole performance a travesty. The regular practice of the Justice Department . . . when an application for pardon was presented was to refer the application to the prosecutor for his comment and recommendations. This young man, however, had sufficient influence to bypass this usual procedure. His father was improperly acquitted and the son was improperly pardoned.

Philip returned to the family store and boredom. A. Musica & Son were in business again. Papa Antonio, avoiding the cheese that had baited the trap, had returned the firm to its original function of purveying a general line of Italian foodstuffs. Cheating the government was evidently not considered much of a crime, for the banks did not hesitate to finance the reopening of the Musica firm. Business was good —good enough to support the style of living to which the Musicas had become accustomed in Bay Ridge.

Philip did not stay long behind the counter. Merchandising macaroni and mozzarella was not enough of a challenge to his capacities or his ambitions. Leaving the operation of the store largely to his father and younger brother Arthur, he spent much of his time re-exploring his old treasure-trove area on the waterfront. He felt no remorse or stigma as a result of his term at Elmira. On the contrary, he regarded his brief incarceration as an unfortunate interruption of his career to be charged to experience. He knew the mistake he had made: he had trusted persons outside his own family. He would not make the same mistake again.

The docks, ships, the sea had a strange fascination for him, although his only ocean voyage had been made as an embryo. He was convinced that foreign trade was his forte, even if his first venture in it had been disastrous. Importing and exporting were the roads to wealth and power—of that he was convinced—and he turned on his charm for new contacts as well as old. He was too impatient to be satisfied with the status quo. He was very much the young man in a hurry.

He had been out of Elmira only a few months when the big inspiration came to him. It is probable that Mama Assunta may have nudged the muse. It is even possible that Papa Antonio may have dropped a hint that contributed to Philip's decision; after all Papa Antonio was a barber of long standing. And the product that Philip had selected as the source of the next Musica fortune from the import-export trade was —human hair!

Women's fashions in the early years of the twentieth century decreed towering pompadours, French rolls, and other balloon-shaped coiffures not attainable by teasing or other techniques of the 1960's. From Mulberry Bend to Peacock Alley women who wanted the chic above-the-ears profile had to stuff their hairdos with rats, puffs, and switches, all made with human hair, all imported from abroad. What, Philip asked himself, was he waiting for?

Human hair imported from Italy and China in marketable lengths and quality sold for as much as $80 a pound. Eighty dollars! What was he doing selling macaroni at A. Musica & Son's Italian Grocery for sixteen *cents* a pound? Why mine coal when there was gold in the same hills?

The United States Hair Company was born.

The ideal lengths of imported human hair ranged from twelve to twenty inches. Philip Musica set up an organization by which he could get those lengths. They were processed in New York before jobbers and wholesalers were allowed to buy. His shrewd buying and shrewder merchandising, plus the hardest, longest hours he had ever spent, opened up foreign as well as domestic markets. The Musicas were on the march again.

The money rolled in. The Musica clan moved from their original Bay Ridge home to a more lavish one, with lawns, gardens, and stables for the horses that Philip's sisters were learning to ride.

Philip himself maintained a permanent suite at the Knickerbocker Hotel in midtown Manhattan. He was back on Broadway with plenty of money to spend, old friendships to brazen out, new friendships to cultivate with an eye to the future. The future was his new credo. The last vestiges of Mulberry Bend were being buffed away. Even the vestiges of his previous Broadway incarnation were getting dim. He was developing new values. As his discernment sharpened, he saw that the moneyed class was not monolithic. He began to perceive the different levels, at first subtle to his naïve eye, but more and more obvious as his sophistication grew. He recalled the poise and the accents of his first hero, Theodore Roosevelt, who had just relinquished the White House, and Diamond Jim Brady began to recede into limbo.

Broadway was joining Mulberry Bend and even Bay Ridge as steppingstones to be discarded. He was learning about new social strata, new status symbols. He discovered Wall Street. He was fascinated by the Social Register. He could distinguish gradations of dress and manner, and he knew which he wanted. He wanted dignity, security, a richness in depth with perhaps just a soupçon of arrogance in contrast to the flamboyance and bluster, the flashy clothes and noisy ostentation that had marked his initiation to expensive living. Cautiously, selectively, he began to cultivate new associations.

Money was pouring into the coffers of A. Musica & Son but it was new money, self-made money, big money only in the scale of a small shopkeeper. It was not to be compared to the sound inherited fortunes of the Social Register or the huge, spectacular fortunes of Wall Street. Since he could not change his heritage—at least at this point in his life he had not yet found a way—he chose Wall Street as his fish pond. His bait was fit only for smelt or minnow, yet he was out to catch the big ones.

In 1912, Philip Musica was only twenty-eight, but he was still in a hurry. He had no time for the slow, steady accumulation of an honest fortune that would be his passport to the world he coveted. He would reach his goal in one tremendous leap. He would become a merchant prince overnight because he was, he was convinced, a financial genius. He could build in months an empire that it would take lesser humans years to create. He would turn the United States Hair Company into a mammoth enterprise that would make the world gasp.

His first step was to send astute Mama Assunta Musica

back to Naples, accompanied by her youngest son, Robert, and her younger daughters, Evelyn and Lucy. As mother of an American captain of big business, she made an impressive repatriate. Her American offspring gave her an aura of respectability. And the letters of introduction which Philip had ingeniously provided her with, gave her entrée into rarefied strata of Neapolitan business and finance. Soon she had set up a salon to entertain the élite of Italian banking and industry, who accepted her without question as the bona fide representative of an important international enterprise with headquarters in New York.

Mama Assunta was ostensibly buying up long and expensive strands of human hair for export to America and other countries. With a talent for chicanery which left no doubt about where Philip's inherited genius came from, she obtained large loans from otherwise canny Italian bankers on the sole security of her invoices for the hair shipments. The bankers failed to take into account the fact that Mama Assunta was the wife of a former Neapolitan barber, and that nothing in her experience on two continents ever went to waste. The crates covered by the invoices that served as security for her loans did indeed contain human hair. But except for a thin layer of the long, expensive lengths for camouflage, the crated hair consisted exclusively of sweepings from the floors of Neapolitan barbershops.

The first phase of Philip's master plan was working like a well-oiled charm. While his mother was pyramiding loans from Italian banks, proving out the techniques of the financial sleight of hand he had devised, Philip set up a network of agents in major cities around the world, including London, Berlin, Hong Kong, St. Petersburg, and Yokohama. These agents were supposedly doing a vast international trade in human hair. Actually they were little more than mail drops for a flow of correspondence—on impressive stationery with the international line-up on the letterheads—about purely imaginary transactions.

In July of 1912, four months after Mama Assunta had started her Italian adventure, the United States Hair Company was incorporated with a capitalization of $2,000,000, listing as assets $600,000 worth of human hair, most of it in inventories abroad. In his New York offices, Philip Musica sat on the throne of his paper empire that stretched around the globe. With deft wizardry he shuttled invoices, letters of credit, drafts, deposits, withdrawals, and loans around the world. And his basic asset, his fictitious inventory of human hair, continued to grow.

Young Musica thought he had discovered a principle that was to be promulgated a quarter-century later by a writer named Adolf Schickelgruber (who used the pen name of A. Hitler): The big lie goes marching on where the tiny fib falls flat on its face. The cynical paraphrase that Musica was trying out was this: a timorously presented rubber check for $10 will arouse the bank president, the board of directors, the American Bankers Association, and the United States Treasury, whereas a bold request for a half-million dollars in credit will evoke only a quick and smiling assent. The major banks of the world, particularly those of New York and London, shuttled huge sums back and forth for the United States Hair Company without a breath of suspicion. Musica was relying on the fact that he had schooled himself well in the intricacies of international banking, whereas the international bankers seemed singularly vague about the fine points of the import-export business.

While Philip Musica was fattening his golden geese for

the kill, he was taking precautions that later escaped the big-lie exponents of Nazi Germany. Having admitted to himself that his intentions were strictly dishonorable, that he was scuttling the slow-but-sure pattern of a sound business venture in favor of a get-rich-quick swindle, he hedged his bets. At the height of his financial flimflam, he purchased a tramp steamer named *Evelyn*, which he registered under the flag of Uruguay. He also bought standard works on international law, particularly books listing the countries having extradition treaties with the United States, the crimes covered by each treaty, and the countries that had no such treaties. He seemed particularly interested in Italy and Honduras as possible havens for a fugitive from American justice.

Philip's timetable did not, however, envisage the immediate use of *Evelyn* as a means of flight. The United States Hair Company was riding high. The ebb and flow of millions through the banking channels of the world worked psychological wonders with Philip's new friends and associates. He was not only recognized personally as a financial wizard, but his United States Hair Company was recognized as a thriving, lucrative enterprise worthy of investment. In October, 1912, U.S. Hair shares were accepted for trading on the New York Curb Exchange. They immediately attracted the attention of speculators looking for speedy growth stocks. Shares climbed quickly from $2 to more than $10.

The day of reckoning seemed so far away that Musica could not bear the thought of *Evelyn* gathering barnacles on her idle bottom. He put her to work as a sort of twentieth-century blackbirder. Her first mission was to transport a consignment of 300 indentured Negroes from Africa to work in the cranberry bogs of Massachusetts.

Then just when the geese were beginning to lay their

golden eggs according to Philip's accelerated schedule, disaster struck once more. On March 11, 1913, less than five months after United States Hair Company stock was first listed on Wall Street, the firm was deep in trouble. Philip Musica was summoned to the offices of the Anglo-South American Trust Company, one of the banks that was financing the Musica enterprises, to explain why two London banks had refused to honor drafts aggregating $135,000 which he had sold to Anglo-South American.

Musica turned on all his charm, smilingly tut-tutted the bankers' fears, and assured them that he would immediately send off cables that should clear up in short order the mistakes of his overseas agents.

He knew, of course, that the jig was up and that it was only a matter of time before his world exploded with a loud bang. He did not panic, however. He set out methodically to salvage everything he could from the wreckage before his paper empire collapsed. And ruin was fast approaching. United States Hair Company shares took a sharp and sudden dip on the Curb Exchange.

Possibly the fate of the U.S.H.C. drafts in London may have started the downward trend, although other reasons were advanced at the time. One theory blamed a suspicious Wall Street trader who recalled the Musica cheese swindle and started a selling wave. Another charged the drop to profit-taking by an impatient group of speculators. Still another attributed the debacle to a group of Wall Street gamblers who, scenting a moment of truth, sold U.S.H.C. stock short.

Musica tried to stem the dizzy downward trend with his own funds, but when he saw that the market was beyond his ability to influence, he made his final plans.

Two days after his contretemps at Anglo-South American, on March 13, 1913, he appeared at the offices of the Bank of the Manhattan Company. With superb effrontery he declared that he had 216 cases of human hair in expensive lengths, worth $370,000, and that he wanted a loan to cover the entire value of the bills of lading and bills of exchange. The Bank of the Manhattan Company took the security but gave Musica only $25,000. He then hurried around to several other banks, using duplicates of the same bills of lading and exchange, and negotiated loans for similar amounts. Between banks he paused to pick up a fortune in diamonds and other jewels from Fifth Avenue firms that had let him take jewelry on approval before. He also converted all current accounts to cash and sent word to his father, two brothers, and two sisters in Bay Ridge: Pack!

Philip's well-laid plans for flight meanwhile struck a snag. His timetable having been upset, his steamer *Evelyn* was at sea when she was needed most. Although Marconi's newfangled wireless telegraph had proved its value during the *Titanic* disaster the previous year, *Evelyn* was not so equipped and was thus beyond communication. Actually, although Philip did not know it at the time, *Evelyn*'s crew had mutinied, put the captain ashore in Bermuda, and was heading for New Bedford. Philip had to make other travel arrangements.

Time was running out. A clerk at the Bank of the Manhattan Company, checking the security for the Musica loan, noted that some figures on one of the bills of lading had apparently been tampered with. He reported to his superiors that a 17 had been made to look like a 77. Immediately men were dispatched to the pier to examine the cases of hair in question. Every case, under a veneer of inferior hair in short lengths, contained barbershop sweepings and old newspapers. The total value of the shipment, instead of $370,000, came to less than $250.

Next day, while Papa Antonio and four of the younger Musicas were busily stripping their Bay Ridge home of valuables, representatives of the firm of Rushmore, Bisbee and Stern, attorneys for the Bank of the Manhattan Company, reached Philip at the Front Street offices of the United States Hair Company and summoned him to explain the shocking disclosure of the worthless hair shipments. Philip declared himself as shocked and mystified as the attorneys. He blandly assured them that he had perfect confidence in his overseas agents, but expressed the suspicion that they had been duped by unscrupulous European suppliers. He immediately dictated cables which, he said he was certain, would clear up the mystery in a day or two.

The attorneys seemed satisfied. They could not know, of course, that while Philip was brazenly talking himself out of immediate trouble, he had in his pocket rail and steamship tickets for six Musicas.

For four days after the London drafts were disclosed to be fraudulent, Philip Musica continued to stride calmly and purposefully through the money lanes of New York, tying up the loose ends of his swindle package. He seemed to enjoy the fragrance of fear, to thrive on the imminence of disaster. Only when he was sure there were no more golden eggs to be collected was he ready to leave the city. On March 15, while various bankers and their legal advisers waited for Philip's promised explanations, the Musicas quietly left New York.

Two more days passed before the bankers, reluctant to believe they had been duped, took belated action. On St. Patrick's Day, Attorney Henry R. Stern, acting for the Bank of the Manhattan Company, asked the district attorney's office to issue warrants for the missing Musicas. On the same day Henry McKenzie, representing the Anglo-South American Bank, obtained a Supreme Court attachment for $134,687 —the amount of the forged drafts on the two London banks. These two legal actions suddenly awakened several other banks, which had been sleeping through the beguiling and soporific palaver of Philip Musica. But by that time there were few Musica assets to attach. The bilked financial giants had little resource except the punitive. The chase was on.

The comedy of errors was also on. Police detectives and private investigators hired by each of the wronged banks were falling all over each other. In a single day five operatives, each working for another Musica victim, ran into and over each other in a frantic search for clues on a trail that was growing colder hour by hour.

The Musicas, however, believed that their pursuers were breathing down the back of their necks. They consequently threw away the two-day lead that Philip's shrewdness had won them. While detectives, public and private, were still sniffing at clues and tripping over each other in Manhattan and Brooklyn, the Musicas were crisscrossing the Eastern seaboard, changing trains and itineraries frequently to shake off the pursuers who were not there, on their way south.

The least befuddled of the detectives was a man named James Downing, who made the unorthodox move of starting at the beginning: the Front Street offices of the U.S. Hair Company. Here a clerk named Philip Papura told Downing he had not seen Musica in five days. Downing then went to Bay Ridge, where an elderly caretaker said he had not seen any of the Musicas in a month (probably an exaggeration). The detective next checked Philip's bachelor *pied-à-terre* at the Knickerbocker Hotel in Manhattan, where he was told that Philip had checked out two days earlier. He also learned that a man named Horst had helped Philip pack (a $12 trunk he had borrowed from Horst) and that Horst had accompanied him to Newark where he boarded a southbound train.

It was at this point that investigators digging in the Front Street offices discovered the manual of extradition laws, with underlined passages in the sections on Italy and Honduras.

Then the William Burns Detective Agency moved in, retained by the American Bankers Association acting on behalf of its members who had been fleeced. The Burns operatives first obtained a detailed description of the trunk Horst had lent to Musica, then traced the trunk through intermediate baggage rooms to Washington, D.C. They also learned that some of the Musica family's bags had been marked with the name "Martin."

When it became apparent that the Musicas were moving in a southerly direction, Burns wired his top southern regional chief, Dan Lehon, to take over. When Lehon heard that a sextet vaguely resembling the Musicas had passed through Atlanta en route to Mobile, he himself rushed to Alabama. He reached Mobile after his quarry had departed, but he learned that Papa Antonio and his two daughters had registered as the Martins, of Hartford, Connecticut, at the centrally located Windsor Hotel, while Philip and his two brothers had registered at an outlying lodging house as William, Roger, and M. Weeks of Chicago.

The cagey Philip had evacuated his family from Mobile by car, boarding a New Orleans-bound train at a whistle stop called Theodore. Lehon skillfully traced their movements, but always several hours behind. He reached New Orleans in the middle of the night, and because Philip was apparently becoming overconfident—the family was still using the names of Martin and Weeks—he ran them down at the Hotel De Soto. Having no legal standing, Lehon called in the New Orleans police to share his stake-out at the hotel.

Next morning, March 19, four days after the Musicas vanished from New York, nine trunks tagged as belonging to "Weeks" and "Martin" were loaded onto a van outside the De Soto. Lehon and the New Orleans police officers followed the van to the United Fruit Company's docks, where the trunks were hoisted aboard the banana steamer *Heredia* scheduled to sail for Honduras ports in a few hours. A short while later, opting for family unity against common-sense caution, the Musicas arrived in a group and boarded the ship.

Checking the passenger list, the police found that Philip and his second sister, Grace, were traveling as Mr. and Mrs. Weeks of Chicago. Papa Antonio, sister Louise, and brothers Arthur and George were all listed under the name of Martin. The police rapped on the door of the cabin occupied by "Mr. and Mrs. Weeks." When Philip refused to open up, they broke down the door.

The rest of the family surrendered meekly at first, but their inborn Neapolitan sense of the dramatic was too strong to allow the occasion to pass without some theatrics. As the Musicas were herded on deck, sister Louise broke away from the policeman holding her arm and dashed for the rail. Plunging her hand into the most intimate recesses of her shirtwaist, she extracted a package that, with an extravagant gesture, she tried to throw overboard. The officer wrenched it from her. It contained $18,000 in currency!

As the Musicas were being marched down the gangplank to the dock, Papa Antonio suddenly reached into Philip's pocket and pulled out a revolver.

"Addio, bambini," he wailed. "I am disgraced. I must kill myself."

"No, Papa! No!" Philip snatched the gun from the old man's hand and pressed it against his own temple. "This is my responsibility, Papa."

The police grabbed the revolver, the moment of hysteria and gestures passed, and the Musicas were driven to police headquarters.

Sister Louise's spectacular nonchalance with the $18,000 inspired a thorough search of the Musicas by policemen and police matrons. The frisking process netted $69,000 in U.S. currency, some of it in thousand-dollar and five-thousand-dollar bank notes, plus $10,000 worth of English and Italian money. The women were wearing jewelry worth $12,000, and Philip carried uncut diamonds worth another several thousand dollars. Philip also carried paid-up life insurance policies with a face value of $225,000.

Arraigned in a New Orleans court as fugitives from justice, Philip as family spokesman waived extradition proceedings. The return of the Musicas to New York City was delayed, however, when Papa Antonio was stricken with a heart attack in the New Orleans jail. For several days his life hung in the balance. Although he recovered sufficiently to return to New York City with his sons and daughters, the shock of the second debacle of Philip's grandiose get-rich-quick schemes was too much for the old man's frail health. He died a few months later.

While criminal proceedings were being prepared against the Musicas, the firm of A. Musica & Son was forced into bankruptcy and Ezra Prentice appointed receiver. The Musicas were represented by a rising young New York attorney named Joseph Force Crater, who seventeen years later was himself to become the center of a *cause célèbre*. In August, 1930, at the beginning of an inquiry into municipal corruption that ended in the resignation of Mayor Jimmie Walker, Joseph Crater, then a New York Supreme Court justice, mysteriously vanished. Unlike the Musicas, Judge Crater was never seen again.

Seventy-eight creditors entered claims in the bankruptcy proceedings. The largest among them were: Anglo-South American Bank, $135,246; Bank of Montreal, $73,141; J. and W. Seligman, $31,141; Brown Brothers, $10,965.

Ezra Prentice was to seek hidden Musica assets for the next ten years, with picayune results. He found that the Musicas were about to branch out into the merchandising of diamonds, but he unearthed no stones. Evidence indicated that Philip had channeled almost a quarter of a million dollars to Mama Assunta in Naples. Hauled into an Italian court, Assunta hotly denied having received more than living expenses. The Musica fiscal operations had been so artfully devised that the shrewdest auditors could not untangle them to prove her wrong. Mama Assunta, however, remained in Naples with children Robert, Evelyn, and Lucy for another two years. Not until the dust had settled did she return to the family mansion in Bay Ridge.

In the cellar of the Musica stables in Bay Ridge, Prentice found several hundred sacks of high-grade human hair, which brought in a few thousand dollars. He located the steamer *Evelyn* in New Bedford, but her sale brought only a fraction of the $25,000 Philip had paid for her.

Among the investigators retained by the banks to trace some Brooklyn property reputedly owned by Philip was an operative of the International Detective Agency, a man named Edward Hubbard. Hubbard was to play a very important part in Philip Musica's life a few years later, but at this first crossing of their paths he was completely stymied. The ownership of the Brooklyn property was so cleverly involved that Hubbard found it impossible to tie it to Philip.

When Philip Musica faced the court to plead to the embezzlement indictment, he repeated his successful performance in the Great Cheese Swindle. He made an eloquent plea for clemency for his family. His was the complete responsibility; the others were guilty of nothing except blind faith in him. He himself was completely innocent of criminal intent. The entire situation could be blamed on "European hair firms which had defrauded the United States Hair Company." He had been the unfortunate victim of forces beyond his capacities. At twenty-eight he had been too young and inexperienced to cope with the complexities of a million-dollar enterprise, too guileless to avoid being duped.

His flight with his family was not an admission of guilt. It had merely been an effort to find the time and means to rehabilitate his own fortunes and to repay the banks he had unwittingly swindled.

"If I had only had a little more time," he told the district attorney, "everything would have been straightened out and every last creditor would have been paid."

The prosecution was impressed. Philip was allowed to plead guilty while charges against his two brothers and his dying father were dropped.

Philip was remanded to the Tombs to await sentencing.

3 : The Bridge of Sighs

NEW YORK'S historic prison called the Tombs was seventy-five years old when Philip Musica moved in to await his sentence. Some of his old neighbors from Mulberry Bend had been executed in its courtyard, more had been incarcerated there, and in 1913 some were still his fellow inmates. In addition to the sorry lot of petty thieves, dope addicts, alcoholics, wife beaters, and pimps, some of the most notorious criminals of the early twentieth century shared his Centre Street address. Philip Musica scorned the hoodlums and pickpockets, but he made use of the big-shot murderers whose notoriety, if properly exploited, might help him achieve his immediate goals.

Philip's plan was simple. Despite his plea of guilty and the overwhelming mass of evidence against him, he was determined not to serve time in the penitentiary. As long as he could delay his sentencing, he would remain in the way station of the Tombs. And as long as he remained in the Tombs he could manipulate characters on both sides of the law to secure his release. After all, had he not been sprung from Elmira by intercession of the President of the United States?

The Tombs prison was connected with the Criminal Courts Building by an overhead passageway, popularly known as the Bridge of Sighs, that allowed prisoners to be brought to court from their cells for arraignment, trial, or sentencing without touching street level. The office of the district attorney for New York County was in the Criminal Courts Building. Musica's problem was to secure an audience with the D.A. and to ingratiate himself so firmly and quickly that he would have free access to the Bridge of Sighs, a great challenge to his powers of persuasion. He had bewitched and bewildered cold-blooded bankers, shrewd lawyers, and hardheaded businessmen, but his seduction of the sophisticated prosecutors of the D.A.'s staff was pure mesmerism.

The district attorney in 1913 was Charles S. Whitman, a bright young man with political ambitions, grooming himself to be governor of New York. Governor William Sulzer was impeached that year, and Lieutenant Governor Martin Glynn, who was finishing out Sulzer's term, could offer little opposition in the 1914 elections in view of the reputation Whitman had achieved for his vigorous prosecution of the Becker-Rosenthal case.

Police Lieutenant Charles Becker, head of the gambling squad, had quarreled with a notorious gambler named Herman Rosenthal. Rosenthal claimed that Becker was a partner in his Broadway casino, and when Mayor Gaynor and Police Commissioner Waldo would not listen to him, he went to District Attorney Whitman. On the night of July 12, 1912, Rosenthal had promised Whitman he would produce documentary proof of his charges against Becker, and a few hours later Rosenthal was shot down by four hired gunmen outside the Metropole, a Times Square hotel. Even without the testimony of his star witness, Big Jack Zelig, who was murdered on a Second Avenue streetcar the day before the trial, Whitman secured the conviction of the four gunmen—Gyp the Blood, Lefty Louie, Dago Frank, and Whitey Lewis. The quartet said they had been hired at the behest of Lieutenant Becker.

Since Becker was in the Tombs awaiting his several trials when Philip Musica took up residence there, Whitman's deputies were not hard to convince that confidential reports from the other end of the Bridge of Sighs might be of great value. Musica became a stool pigeon for the D.A.'s office.

Being far from an ordinary man, Musica was not an ordinary stool pigeon either. Most stoolies are despised by their employers as well as by the people they betray. Not so Musica. He was eminently respected on both sides of the bridge. To his fellow prisoners, instead of a cowering rat living in constant fear of vengeance from a kangaroo court, he was a big shot con man, a million-dollar swindler who stole only from the pillars of an affluent society. He was a boy from Mulberry Bend who had made high marks in crime, and so they were sure that his good graces with the enemy across the bridge would be used only on their behalf. He was one of the royalty of crime.

To the prosecutors at the other end of the Bridge of Sighs, Musica was a brilliant young businessman who was repenting a mistake. His success in winning the confidence and sympathy of the D.A.'s staff can be exemplified by the testimony of Assistant District Attorney Alfred L. Becker (no kin of the ex-Lieutenant), at a Senate hearing some years later: "I have watched the conduct of Musica since he came to my office. . . . I have been convinced there is such a thing as reform. I know his past. I know how hard he has worked to make good. I stand by him. I am his friend."

Musica's friendship with the D.A.'s office was undoubtedly useful, even though it was based strictly on self-interest. When it became apparent that the feud between Mayor Gaynor and the district attorney's office was being carried on by the newly elected Mayor John Purroy Mitchel, Musica decided it would be good politics (as well as personally advantageous) to embarrass the mayor and his commissioner of correction with a nice, juicy scandal in the Tombs. He drew up a simple five-line complaint about the quality of the food being served the prisoners and enlisted the help of ex-Police Lieutenant Becker to circulate it as a petition. When 319 prisoners signed, Musica stripped off the top sheet with its innocuous five-line protest against the prison cuisine and substituted four typewritten pages of violent attack on the administration of the Tombs by Dr. Katherine B. Davis, commissioner of correction. He made sure that the petition, which charged graft and corruption, reached the press.

When Dr. Katherine Davis questioned Musica about the petition, he blandly denied having anything to do with it. He accused ex-Lieutenant Becker of having written and circulated it. His denial was contradicted both inside and out. Dr. Davis made a public statement charging Musica with instigating the plot to gain favor in Albany and with Tammany Hall. A long-time acquaintance of Musica's, Philip Saitta, a lawyer awaiting sentence on a grand larceny conviction, told the press: "It was Musica who got the petition up, not Becker. He hoped to curry favor with the district attorney by doing everything in his power to prejudice the public against Becker." Saitta also pointed out that "Musica was convicted over a year ago and he is still here in the Tombs . . . by pulling such rotten contemptible things as this. He boasts openly that he has more pull than anyone else here."

Under pressure, Musica admitted his part in the petition. The incident had obviously made him enemies, but it had strengthened friendships in places that mattered most to him.

Ex-Lieutenant Becker was found guilty of murder in the first degree. Not surprisingly, he was denied clemency by Governor Charles S. Whitman, who as district attorney had prosecuted him. He was executed at Sing Sing on July 30, 1915.

On that date Philip Musica was still in the Tombs, still unsentenced.

Musica's career as courier and confidant for both ends of the Bridge of Sighs was marked by false affidavits, devious practices, perfidy, and a deep strain of malice. Even his offers of help to his fellow prisoners were tainted with cynicism and treachery. That he escaped retribution at the hands of some kangaroo court is added testimony to the persuasive charm which was the explanation of an otherwise incredible career.

One of his most blatant acts of perfidy was his relationship with Hans Schmidt, a bogus priest charged with the murder of a servant girl. The case, which continued through most of Musica's stay in the Tombs, was New York's crime of the year for 1913.

On September 2 of that year a striped pillowcase fished from the Hudson River was found to contain the upper part of a woman's torso. The only clue was a tag on the pillowcase bearing the name of the maker, Robertson-Roder Company, Newark, New Jersey, and the number "89." Inspector Joseph Faurot, one of the top detectives of the New York City police, took over. When he learned that the complete line of that size and pattern pillowcase had been absorbed by

George Sachs, an Eighth Avenue furniture dealer, Inspector Faurot fanned out his men to check every purchaser.

Every address except a flat on Bradhurst Avenue proved unrewarding. After a five-day stake-out on Bradhurst Avenue, Inspector Faurot entered with the superintendent's key and was convinced he had found the scene of a murder. Bloodstains on the floor and walls had resisted the scrub brush. There was no bedding. A butcher knife and handsaw were found in one trunk, a letter addressed to one Anna Aumüller in the other. The superintendent told Inspector Faurot that the flat had been rented by one H. Schmidt for a "young woman relative."

The girl's name led the police to the rectory of St. Boniface, where Anna had worked as a servant. The pastor told the inspector that a Reverend Hans Schmidt had been "connected" with the rectory during the period of the girl's employment, but that he had moved on to St. Joseph's. Aroused at midnight, "Father" Schmidt at first denied knowing Anna Aumüller, then broke down and shouted hysterically: "Yes, I killed her. I killed her because I loved her. Sacrifices should be consummated in blood."

To the district attorney, Schmidt said he had married the girl a few months before the murder, performing the ceremony himself. The marriage license was in order, and he had given her a ring, but he was forced to kill her to prove the sanctity of their love "by the blood rite."

Inspector Faurot's investigation uncovered a personality as complex and chameleonic as Musica himself. Schmidt the spurious priest (St. Joseph's) and Schmidt the lover (Broadhurst Avenue) had still another identity: Schmidt the counterfeiter. In an apartment on West 134th Street police found an elaborate setup of color presses, engraving plates, cameras, and stacks of ten-dollar bills that were extremely skillful facsimiles. They also found that Schmidt sometimes posed as a Dr. Emil Molière, a Paris surgeon, and that he did a thriving business in forged diplomas for German universities.

When the amazing Schmidt was ushered into the Tombs, he was immediately impressed and beguiled by the even more amazing Philip Musica. In his dank cell on Centre Street, Schmidt began to wonder if his hysteria on arrest had done him any good. After all, he was being charged with a capital crime, and he had no particular desire to indulge in any sacrificial rites of his own. He confided in his new friend.

Schmidt told Musica the whole story of his romance with Anna Aumüller. He had become involved with her soon after he went to St. Boniface's. She became pregnant almost immediately. He financed a trip to Austria for an abortion that he arranged by mail with some former associates.

When she returned, they resumed their relationship. It was not long before she was again big with child and, this time, with doubts. She questioned his curious dual status as priest and layman. She insisted on marriage. When he doubled as groom *and* officiating clergyman, Anna became even more suspicious. Schmidt insisted on another abortion, to be performed in the Bradhurst Avenue flat with the assistance of a friend. The operation was botched and the girl died.

Schmidt purchased a large butcher knife and a saw and proceeded to reduce Anna to convenient parcels, which could be stuffed into pillowcases or wrapped in sheets. He dropped the gruesome packages into the Hudson during four trips on the Fort Lee ferry.

"What do I do now, Mr. Musica? I don't want to die."

Musica promised to devise a defense for the bogus priest. He knew he had to work fast because, although "Father"

Schmidt had made a father confessor of Musica almost at first sight, a coroner's inquest was scheduled as soon as pathologists could assemble enough of the disjointed fractions of Anna to perform a meaningful autopsy. Musica crossed the Bridge of Sighs to borrow a set of statutes from the D.A.'s office and after a cursory study advised Schmidt to lay the basis for a plea of insanity.

The coroner's inquest—New York City was still five years away from supplanting its politics-ridden coroner's office with the medical examiner system—would be a dress rehearsal for his plea. Musica coached Schmidt in a series of antics that would be reported by the press, and thus excite the sympathy of prospective jurors when the case came to trial.

The coroner's jury included a panel of well-known citizens: Vincent Astor; Marcus Loew, the theater magnate; and Theodore Shonts, president of the Interborough Rapid Transit subway system in New York City. The public and the press turned out en masse. The coroner's quarters could not contain the crowd and the inquest was moved to the Court of General Sessions.

Schmidt was all primed to demonstrate his mental instability. When the coroner referred to the insolvency of the deceased and remarked that Anna would have to be buried in Potter's Field unless some generous soul came forward to assure her a decent funeral, Schmidt took this as a cue for his mad scene. He rose to his feet, looked wildly at the spectators, then drew handfuls of coins and rosary beads from his pocket to fling into the crowd. The surprised gasps had scarcely subsided when he drew out more coins, looking for targets. Attendants wrestled him back into his seat.

Despite the exhibition, the coroner's jury found that Anna Aumüller had come to her death "wilfully and feloniously at

the hands of one Hans Schmidt." The prisoner's wild out-
burst, however, was widely reported in the press, and Musica
urged Schmidt to go on feigning insanity.

"Look at Harry K. Thaw," said Musica. "He couldn't very
well deny he shot Stanford White since he did it in Madison
Square Garden. But he beat the chair, didn't he?" It was
seven years since Thaw, a Pittsburgh millionaire, had killed
the architect White over his alleged attentions to Thaw's
wife, Evelyn Nesbitt Thaw, but everyone remembered that
Thaw had been sent, not to Sing Sing, but to Matteawan,
New York's institution for the criminally insane.

To bolster his argument, Musica turned over to Schmidt
the borrowed lawbooks in which he had marked the passages
dealing with the legal aspects of insanity. He also prompted
Schmidt to give his peculiar conduct newsworthy aspects. A
fellow prisoner became hysterical with fear after spending a
night in the same cell with Schmidt and demanded protection because Schmidt had threatened to kill him in a religious
rite that would wash away his sins with blood.

Schmidt's father came from Germany to testify to the
strange conduct of the accused as a boy. Defense alienists con-
tended that Schmidt was suffering from dementia precox.
Prosecution psychiatrists found him sane and shamming.

Schmidt's antics were more subdued during the trial, but
they apparently convinced two jurors. After thirty-four hours
of deliberation and countless ballots, the foreman informed
the court that it was impossible to reach a decision, that the
jurors were hopelessly deadlocked on a vote of ten to two for
conviction. The jury was dismissed.

During the second trial, Musica tipped off the prosecution
that Schmidt had been studying the laws pertaining to insanity in criminal cases. When the books Musica had marked

up and lent to Schmidt were found in the bogus priest's cell and placed in evidence, they constituted such damaging exhibits that they practically sealed the defendant's doom. After more than two years in and out of court, Schmidt was found guilty and sentenced to death.

There were several stays of execution to permit appeals, which were denied. In a final attempt to escape the electric chair, Schmidt wrote to both Governor Whitman and the new district attorney for New York County (Whitman's successor), admitting that he had feigned insanity. He confessed to responsibility for Anna Aumüller's pregnancy and for the abortion that had resulted in her accidental death. His insanity defense, he asserted, had been conceived by his false friend Philip Musica.

The letter prompted Governor Whitman to grant a thirty-day reprieve to allow one more appeal. The appeal was rejected by Justice Benjamin Cardozo, later to be elevated to the U.S. Supreme Court, who ruled that a false defense in a murder trial, in any case, represents the defendant's complete right to a day in court. If, instead of heeding Musica's advice, Schmidt had admitted his guilt as an amateur abortionist whose bungling had caused the death of his mistress, he might well have escaped with a conviction for manslaughter, or at most for second-degree murder. A first-degree murder conviction then carried a mandatory death penalty unless the jury recommended mercy or the governor exercised his executive clemency.

Governor Whitman refused clemency and Hans Schmidt died in the electric chair at Sing Sing in March, 1916.

Within a few days of the execution, Philip Musica was given a suspended sentence, placed on probation, and walked out of the Tombs a free man.

4 : William Johnson, Special Investigator

Almost immediately upon his release from the Tombs, ex-prisoner Philip Musica was hired at $25 a day as a special investigator for the Office of the Attorney General of the State of New York.

This surprising appointment came partly as a reward for Musica's faithful service as Tombs informer for the D.A.'s office, partly because his special knowledge of the underworld gained during three years of imprisonment was believed to be of value to Governor Whitman in a current investigation, but mostly because Musica had his own chicken to fry in the bloody civil war going on in the poultry markets of Manhattan.

The poultry war became a shooting war three weeks after District Attorney Charles S. Whitman had been elected governor. On Thanksgiving Eve, 1914, Barnet Baff, a millionaire chicken dealer who had been fighting the so-called "poultry trust," was shot dead in West Washington Market. It was page-one news for days, because the vicious rivalry between groups of poultry dealers had been going on for some time. When, a year and a half after Baff had been shot to death among his Thanksgiving turkeys, the murder had not yet been solved, Governor Whitman felt that the glory that had accrued to him from the Becker and Schmidt convictions might be beginning to dim. The investigation was too long, too expensive, and too unproductive. So the governor appointed one of his bright young men, aggressive attorney Albert L. Becker, as special deputy attorney general with responsibility for solving the Baff murder. Alfred Becker took on as assistants, in addition to Philip Musica, Henry Unterweiser, an attorney, and Benjamin Simon, a shrewd young process server who was to share in Musica's strange career for the next twenty years. Unterweiser's memory of his associate as he was when fresh from the Tombs was to be an important factor during Musica's time of crisis two decades later.

Musica became a special investigator for the attorney general's office under the name of William Johnson. Only three times a month did he admit to the name of Philip Musica— once when he reported to his probation officer in accordance with the terms of his suspended sentence, and twice when he collected his pay from the State of New York. Otherwise he used the antiseptic name of William Johnson.

The background of the Baff murder extended over at least three years. Basically it seemed to be a vendetta between two rival groups of poultry dealers: the Live Poultry Association of West Washington Market (to which Baff himself belonged), a prosperous group which was largely Jewish-dominated; and a shopkeepers' organization, centered in Little Italy, which the West Washington people called "the poultry trust."

When thirteen members of the "trust" were sent to jail on information furnished by Barnet Baff, war was declared. Baff received a number of threats the press called "Black Hand letters." His store was bombed, his chickens stolen, and his horses poisoned. His partner and his son were blackjacked. When A. T. Pierson, No. 2 man in the West Washington Market chicken business (his firm was capitalized at $1,500,-000), joined the fight against the "poultry trust," thugs invaded his place of business and beat him unmercifully.

The Thanksgiving Eve murder saw Baff shot down while talking turkey with customers on the sidewalk of Third Street near Thompson Street, a few steps from his poultry emporium, by gunmen who fired through a thicket of chicken crates and escaped in an automobile.

The same Inspector Faurot who had cracked the Schmidt case was assigned to the Baff murder. Early indications pointed to professional assassins hired by Antonio Cardinale, a poultry dealer who ran with the Little Italy chicken men. Cardinale had once accused Baff of salting his chickens with gravel to increase their weight. According to tips reaching Faurot, the assassins had been paid off by Ippolito Gresco, who owned a tavern in Italian East Harlem. Before Faurot could check his information, Gresco had been murdered in a stable behind his bar and Cardinale had fled to Italy.

Suddenly the investigation veered off on a new tack. Six days after Baff was murdered, the police picked up a chicken inspector named Harry Cohen, alias Kid Griffo. Later, the police arrested Harry's older brother Joseph, a poultry trucker with an unsavory record, and another brother, Jacob, in connection with the beating of Pierson.

The arrest of the Cohens was masterminded by Musica. He claimed to have wormed the story out of Carl Rettich, a Hoboken bartender who had been held in the Tombs overnight during Musica's stay there. Rettich had allegedly heard the Cohens plotting to have James Moore, one of their drivers, attack Pierson. The conspirators, said Musica, had been overheard in Rettich's bar, a hangout for big chicken-and-turkey people.

Shortly after Philip Musica became William Johnson, special investigator, the Baff case took another turn, veering away from the Cohens again. Frank Ferrara, a young East Harlem plumber, confessed to driving the getaway car after the Baff murder. He named Giuseppe Archiello, a hoodlum with a record, as the trigger man. According to Ferrara, they had been paid $100 each. Arrested with these two were Antonio and Giuseppe Zafarano, brothers identified as lookouts. The New York D.A. asked the State Department to start extradition proceedings against Cardinale, who had been located serving as a corporal in the Italian army.

Things were looking dark again for the chicken men of Little Italy, so the boy from Mulberry Bend went into action. Investigator Johnson (*né* Musica) induced one Joseph Sorro, another fellow inmate of the Tombs, to sign an affidavit stating that he had heard Joseph Cohen hiring the killers in an East Harlem saloon. He also provided Ferrara and Archiello with affidavits attesting to their presence elsewhere when the murder was committed. A trip to Sing Sing to get two convicts to testify against Cohen was unsuccessful.

Ferrara and Archiello were eventually released, but Cohen went to trial on a charge of first-degree murder. Sorro's affidavit apparently weighed heavily against him. Cohen was found guilty and sentenced to death. The successful skulduggery by which Musica-Johnson had sent Cohen to the death house could not have been a personal victory, for he scarcely knew Cohen. Rather it was a tribal victory, a triumph for the alumni of Mulberry Bend.

Joseph Cohen, however, refused to give up. From his death cell in Sing Sing, he continued for years to fight for his life. A persistent series of legal maneuvers won reprieve after reprieve. One stay of execution came just in the nick of time. His head had been shaved and his trousers slit. Seven minutes later he would have been dead.

Cohen's tenacity and his story attracted the attention of Ferdinand Pecora, named assistant district attorney for New York County after the election of Governor Alfred E. Smith in 1918. The brilliant Pecora had no trouble in stripping bare the chicanery of Musica-Johnson. Under Pecora's rapier-like questions, Joseph Sorro confessed that the affidavit naming Cohen was a complete fabrication, invented by Musica-Johnson and signed under his urging.

In 1921, Pecora brought Sorro before Judge John Mulqueen on a charge of perjury. He put Musica-Johnson and former Deputy Attorney General Alfred L. Becker on the stand and made them squirm under his verbal flogging. He accused Becker, who had returned to private practice, of having turned over prosecution documents to Sorro's attorney, tipping off the defense to the state's case. He called Musica-Johnson the evil genius behind the plot to railroad an innocent man to the electric chair.

Sorro was convicted of perjury and sent to prison. Musica-Johnson was indicted for subornation of perjury, but such were his unfailing charm and devious machinations that he was never brought to trial. Eight years later the indictment had mysteriously disappeared. So, equally mysteriously, had the files on the Baff case and the records of the U.S. Hair Company swindle.

Seven years after the unsolved murder of Barnet Baff, Attorney Jonah Goldstein persuaded Governor Nathan Miller to pardon Cohen in view of Sorro's confessed perjury. Cohen was freed, but so complex was the fabric of lies and machinations that Musica-Johnson had woven, that the original mystery of the Baff murder was never really unraveled. The repercussions, however, lasted for eleven years after Cohen's release, and there are some who believe that Musica-Johnson was responsible for the final sensation.

On the evening of April 9, 1932, Joseph Cohen was playing cards with his wife, Mina, at their home at 240 Westminster Road, Brooklyn, when the front doorbell rang. Cohen put down his cards and went to open the door. Three men stood there. They pumped nine bullets into his body, saw him fall dead, and ran. They were never caught.

During the years that Cohen had been languishing in the death house, Musica-Johnson was busy establishing himself as a superpatriot, hoping to wipe out the last vestiges of the stigma of having been a Tombs stool pigeon. The United States had been at war with Germany since April 6, 1917 (a little more than a year after the boy from Mulberry Bend was released), the conscription act had been passed five weeks later, and an epidemic of war hysteria had gripped the country. Musica-Johnson was having a field day running down suspected spies and spotting draft dodgers for New York State's attorney general.

He made an impressive record, duly acknowledged by his superiors. His success he owed in large measure to the same underworld pipelines that had served him in the Tombs. His files bulged with the names of young hoodlums to whom the army was even more distasteful than honest work.

Congress had passed drastic espionage and sedition laws, and the execution of those laws reviewed in the cold, clear light of postwar reason was often shocking. Loyal Americans of German descent were slandered and persecuted. A mere Teutonic name was suspicious. Hamburgers became Liberty steaks, German silver became nickel alloy, Wagner's music was hissed, and Rhine wine and Seltzer was an unpatriotic drink. People were hauled into court on the most trivial charges. Almost 2,000 were indicted for disloyal utterances. Eugene V. Debs went to Leavenworth for ten years as much for having been five times the Socialist candidate for president as for his public opposition to war. Agents and investigators used the sedition laws for personal revenge, spite, and malice.

Musica-Johnson was such an agent. He had never forgiven the Hearst newspapers for their sensational treatment of the two major Musica swindles. Now, with the authority of his investigative office behind him, he saw a chance to even old scores. He would destroy William Randolph Hearst.

Hearst had laid himself wide open on the question of pro-German sympathies. Although he insisted he was merely following the policy of strict neutrality proclaimed by President Wilson and his then Secretary of State, William Jennings Bryan, Hearst failed to sense the revulsion of the American people to the sinking of the Cunard liner *Lusitania* on May 7, 1915. The *Lusitania* was torpedoed without warning by a German submarine off the south coast of Ireland, and sank in eighteen minutes with the loss of 1,198 lives, 124 of them American citizens. President Wilson, more sensitive to public opinion than was Hearst, sent off a sharp note to Germany, thus causing the resignation of pacifist Bryan. Hearst, however, seemed to echo the German line (that the *Lusitania* was armed and carried munitions of war) when he editorialized in his New York *American* on June 6, 1915:

> Whether the *Lusitania* was armed or not it was properly a spoil of war subject to attack and destruction under the accepted rules of so-called civilized warfare.

The Lord of San Simeon was curiously insensitive to the horror of the American people at the fact that the U-boat commander had not given warning so that lifeboats could have been lowered. The *Lusitania,* although it may have been carrying a few hundred cases of cartridges among its regular cargo, was primarily a passenger ship, and the ruthless drowning of nearly 1,200 passengers was a characteristically stupid act of German policy, which Mr. Hearst just as stupidly defended.

The gallows tree on which Musica-Johnson planned to hang William Randolph Hearst was a vaguely-Levantine character named Bolo Pasha, a man who had an apparent history of Paris publishing but who, since the outbreak of World War I, had been the No. 1 German propagandist in the United States. Before 1917, his mission had been to swing American sentiment away from the Allies, and to prevent, if possible, the entry of the United States into the war against Germany. In this mission, he would naturally seek the support of the Hearst papers, and there is little doubt that Bolo Pasha did have personal contact with Hearst in his effort to encourage the Hearst campaign to keep America out of Europe's wars.

Musica-Johnson pulled out all stops in an effort to tie William Randolph Hearst in with Bolo Pasha's activities. Even considering a few editorials, there was little evidence that Mr. Hearst's editorial policy was dictated by his association with German officials rather than by his stubborn and bitter hatred of the British because of real or imagined slights in the past. Johnson's vindictiveness, however, refused to take into consideration the fact that any newspaper publisher was a natural target for propagandists from both sides. He was out to get Mr. Hearst.

An old hand at falsifying documents, Special Investigator Johnson turned up with affidavits signed by chauffeurs, doormen, and hotel bellboys alleging that the affiants had seen Bolo Pasha and German Ambassador Von Bernstorff enter Hearst's Riverside Drive home on several occasions during the spring of 1916, almost a year after the sinking of the *Lusitania*.

Johnson's efforts to discredit Hearst were not without some success. At a Madison Square Garden meeting, 5,000 persons cheered the Reverend William T. Manning, Rector of Trinity Church, when he said of Hearst: "Throughout the war, he has been Germany's most useful friend." When New York's Mayor John Hylan named Publisher Hearst to a subcommittee of a "Committee to Welcome the Troops," there was a great hue and cry.

But Musica-Johnson had overplayed his hand. Many people were shocked by the hysteria and malice fomented by the vicious campaign to pillory Hearst. And the publisher's influential friends—apparently more numerous at this time than Musica's—rallied to his defense. Foremost of these was U.S. Senator James A. Reed of Missouri, chairman of the Senate Judiciary Committee. Early in January, 1919, Senator Reed called for hearings on the subject of wartime espionage. The subject was, of course, a blanket subterfuge to destroy the credibility of Hearst's detractors and to rehabilitate the patriotism of the Lord of San Simeon.

As far as William Johnson (*né* Musica) was concerned, the Senator scored a bull's-eye on both targets. Reed quickly made the record show that the affidavits damaging to Hearst had been procured by an investigator who had previously pleaded guilty to charges of grand larceny. This much was admitted by Deputy Attorney General Alfred L. Becker, who faced the Senate committee for several hours.

"Is the real name of this man Musica or Johnson?" Senator Reed demanded.

"I decline to answer," said Becker angrily. There was a stir at the press table.

"If this man Musica, alias Johnson," Senator Reed continued, his voice rising, "is a convict and a notorious criminal, it bears on every phase of this question."

To the Senator's question as to Musica's pay, Becker replied that it had originally been $25 a day, expenses included, but that it had subsequently been changed to $20, plus expenses as vouchered.

Reed then described a wide circle around the Hearst matter to mount a flank attack on Hearst-detractor Musica's integrity and credibility. "Was it not the theory of this man Musica in the Baff case, that it was not the defendants Archiello and Ferrara, who had confessed, but a man named Cohen who was the real murderer? Cohen was convicted and is now under sentence of death—is that true?"

"The theory that Cohen was the man was proved!" Becker insisted heatedly.

"Musica was in touch with Cardinale, the man who put the blame on Cohen," Senator Reed pursued. "You and Musica succeeded in getting Cohen convicted. The original defendants went scot-free."

"That is about fifty percent right," Becker admitted. Under further questioning, he also admitted that the men who procured the affidavits connecting Hearst with Bolo Pasha and Von Bernstorff were employed by Musica.

Musica's phenomenal gift for winning deep loyalties while feeling none himself was again displayed in these Senate hearings. When Reed began to belabor Musica as a despicable criminal and character assassin, Becker leaped to his defense. Musica was truly a reformed character, he said, with tears in his eyes. "I am his friend and I shall continue to be."

Senator Reed's scathing attack was printed in detail by the New York papers, thus ending the usefulness of Philip Musica to the office of the state's attorney general. Also destroyed was Musica's false identity as William Johnson, special investigator.

Unfortunately the name Musica was not quite dead and buried. It was to pop up again two years later during the Sorro perjury trial in 1921, when Musica himself was indicted for subornation of perjury. Never again, however, would the boy from Mulberry Bend—until the last day of his life—be publicly identified as Philip Musica.

5 : Frank D. Costa,
Manufacturing Druggist

WHEN he cleaned out his desk and left the New York attorney general's office early in January, 1919, Philip Musica was thirty-four years old. He had hoped to stay on a little longer, at least until he could establish himself as William Johnson, erasing forever the stigmatized name of Musica before returning to private (and more lucrative) enterprise. Senator Reed, however, had short-circuited that plan.

He was casting about desperately for a design for living that would fit a twice-jailed swindler, a stool pigeon, a forger of affidavits, and a discredited investigator, when he met two men who were to play important parts in his business career and his emotional life. The two men could not have been more unlike. One was Giuseppe Brandino, an unsavory thug and a fellow alumnus of the Tombs. The other was a former private investigator, Edward W. Hubbard, who in 1913 had been one of the pack trying unsuccessfully to run down the Musica assets after the hair swindle.

Brandino had been held in the Tombs on a suspicion of murder in 1915, but he had not been indicted. He left the jail with a deep admiration for the suavity, astuteness, and intelligence of his fellow inmate Philip Musica. When he got out, Brandino joined forces with a brother and two sisters to open a florist shop in Brooklyn. Business prospered, but Brandino was not made for slow, steady, honest advancement. He had an idea for making a lot of money in a hurry. He and his sister Mary had a little money to invest, but they were aware of their own lack of education and worldliness. If they could find a man with brains, talent, and *savoir-faire*—a man like Philip Musica—they would have it made. Congress had just legislated into being a class of prospective newly rich who had only yesterday been little better than the scum of the earth. Brandino knew he could belong if only he could borrow the brains and charm of Philip Musica.

On January 16, 1919, Nebraska had become the thirty-sixth state to ratify the Eighteenth Amendment to the Constitution, and Prohibition would become effective a year later. The Volstead Act, to enforce the amendment, was passed by Congress in October, 1919, and vetoed by President Wilson. Passed over the President's veto, it went into effect on January 17, 1920.

Henceforth no law-abiding citizen would be allowed to buy, sell, or drink intoxicating liquor, so millions of Americans who had never before violated even a local no-parking ordinance became avid customers of the kingdom of crime. In this new imminent gold rush, the Brandinos saw opportunity for personal gain, and Philip Musica saw a new approach to the future he wanted.

Philip Musica was not the kind of man who would build a forbidden still in some sordid hole in the wall. This was not his style. Moreover, he was not one who would join the hood-lums of every stratum who rushed into the race for the money of millions of thirsty Americans rising in revolt against a constitutional amendment. He had twice lost his fight with the law, and he was not going to be an overt part of the thirteen-year binge of cynicism and immorality which was to leave deep scars on the American body politic. He would stand apart from the sleazy combines of speakeasies, the gangster wars, the underworld fleets of rumrunners. Philip Musica would dip his deft fingers into the golden stream, but he would do so respectably and, to all appearances, legally.

Early in 1920, Philip Musica, alias William Johnson, be-came Frank D. Costa.

Early in 1920, Frank Costa started the Adelphi Pharma-ceutical Manufacturing Company on Adelphi Street in Brooklyn. President of the new firm was Benjamin Simon, who had worked with Musica-Johnson-Costa on the New York attorney general's staff during the Baff murder inquiry. Simon was the front for the business. The financing was pro-vided by the Brandinos, who had a little capital and enough bootlegging friends to provide an initial customers' list. Frank Costa was to provide the brains.

Costa's *modus operandi* was simple and fairly safe. Adel-phi Pharmaceutical manufactured hair tonic and cosmetics, ostensibly for the general trade. All its products had a legal, although loaded, alcoholic content. The fact that most, if not all, of its customers found it desirable and lucrative to distill the alcohol out of Adelphi products was no concern of the company's. The company had a perfectly legal government permit to draw 5,000 gallons of denatured alcohol a month for the manufacture of hair tonic and kindred products, which were properly packaged and sold at a profit. The fact that some customers paid an abnormally high price for hair tonic while the company's books showed only the normal competitive price was a matter of private bookkeeping.

Adelphi was soon producing at capacity, and business was booming. At the outset, Costa depended upon the Brandinos for their contacts with smalltime bootleggers, but before long he was developing a weightier clientele of his own. He was, as always, a quick study. He had never envisaged Adelphi, particularly in partnership with the Brandinos, as more than a convenient source of capital and a laboratory for testing bigger ideas.

The partnership had from the start been a marriage of convenience. Costa and the Brandinos needed each other, but they had little in common except the desire for money. There was no love lost between them. The Brandinos were crude, ignorant, and greedy. They had never fully emerged from the big-city jungle. They were openly proud of being feared as potential killers; hadn't Brandino beaten a rap on suspicion of murder? The Brandino-Costa relationship was predestined to be brief. That the suavely intelligent Costa-Musica sweated out the partnership for two years was probably due to the fact that it coincided with Philip's prearranged timetable.

Costa-Musica was already putting out feelers in at least one other direction. He had renewed his relationship with Edward W. Hubbard, who had abandoned his career of private investigator for the greener fields of Wall Street. Hubbard was a nephew of Elbert Hubbard, cultist, moralist, and philosopher, editor of the intellectually slanted *Philistine,* author of the inspirational essay, "Carry a Message to Garcia." Son of a wealthy New York family, Edward Hubbard had been privately educated and had traveled about the world with his own tutor. He had planned a legal career, but when his father died and his mother lost most of her inheritance in bad investments, he became what years later came to be known as a private eye. However, from the outset his investigations were specialized. He opened an office in Wall Street, and his clients were for the most part lawyers, brokers, and corporations.

While on a job for the Long Island Railroad, Edward Hubbard hired a stenographer from a real-estate office to type some reports for him. Her name was Carol Jenkins, daughter of a Brooklyn policeman. She was strikingly pretty, and although she was not yet twenty, she was possessed of a mature intelligence that impressed Hubbard almost as much as her deceptively childlike beauty. A few months after he first met her, Hubbard broke off his engagement to another girl and proposed marriage.

Carol accepted—conditionally. Those big wondering eyes of hers could see far, wide, and shrewdly, even when they were half obscured by her long dark lashes. She loved Ed Hubbard, of course, but wouldn't it be better for both their sakes if they waited until his new venture was a sure thing and they could face the future together with confidence? Hubbard could only admire her common sense. They waited for two years. They were married in 1912, the year before Hubbard's first ill-starred crossing of Musica's path.

When Musica-Costa again came into Hubbard's life in 1919, the ex-investigator was a partner in the brokerage firm of Clarke and Hubbard, members of the Curb Exchange. The brokerage business was flourishing, a fact that naturally attracted the boy from Mulberry Bend. Curiously enough, the dazzle of Hubbard's financial success was not nearly so attractive to Philip Musica as was the quiet glow of Mrs.

Hubbard's charm. For perhaps the only time in his life, Philip Musica was really hooked romantically.

The first time he saw Carol Hubbard, the policeman's daughter was swathed in all the embellishments to her femininity that fashion decreed and Wall Street money could provide. Her big hat, its brim upturned like her little-girl's nose, was piled high with ostrich plumes. Her dark *tailleur* was padded in the shoulders and provocatively pinched in at the waist. The stylishly high collar of her shirtwaist was circled with a choker of pearls and modestly fastened in front with a large black bow. She wore a white fox fur over one shoulder.

In her presence, Philip Musica was painfully aware of how superficial was his veneer of gentility. To him, Carol Hubbard represented all that was gracious in life, all that was desirable in a woman. When she lowered her long lashes demurely over her perpetually dreaming eyes, she was expressing the mystery of her sex that had somehow escaped Musica until that moment.

Once he made up his mind that Carol Jenkins Hubbard was the missing ingredient needed to complete the full life he had set his heart upon, the Hubbard marriage was doomed and Hubbard was already a dead duck. Musica went about his intrigue slowly and methodically. He turned on his charm for Carol with great caution, for he was determined that none of the crassness of Mulberry Bend should show through. And for his campaign to eliminate Hubbard, he chose the oblique approach.

While still keeping things under control at Adelphi, Musica-Costa managed to spend considerable time in Hubbard's brokerage office. Ingratiating himself with Hubbard, he showed a deep interest in the stock brokerage business. It was not long before he wormed himself into a position as adviser and accountant for Clarke and Hubbard. That Hubbard, knowing of Costa's previous incarnations as Musica and Johnson, should have shown such confidence in the man is further evidence of Musica's amazing personal magnetism. With access to the Clarke and Hubbard books, Musica-Johnson-Costa soon had enough confidential data tucked away in his malicious memory to put the partnership at his mercy. The relationship also gave him ample opportunity to pursue his subtle courtship of Carol Hubbard.

The deadline Musica had set himself for the final severance of all his ties with the past was 1922. His two-pronged campaign had twin goals: to separate himself from the Brandinos and to separate Carol from Edward Hubbard. He pursued both with equally ruthless efficiency. By 1922 he would have enough capital to move on to the next stage of his avatar. The destruction of the Clarke and Hubbard brokerage firm and of the Adelphi Pharmaceutical Manufacturing Company would be accomplished simultaneously. The winning of Carol Jenkins Hubbard was to be a tender by-product of the cold-blooded murder of two business enterprises and perhaps the people connected with them.

While Edward Hubbard was in the West on a business trip, Costa-Musica started a series of rumors implying that Clarke was trying to knife his partner during his absence. He induced several friends of Hubbard's to write letters to him, warning of this potential treachery.

When Hubbard returned to New York, Costa played variations on the theme, amplifying the rumors to strike shrewdly at the soft spots in his victim's sensitive, high-strung personality. Slowly but methodically he dripped acid into the now-vulnerable relationship between Clarke and Hubbard.

When the erosion seemed too slow, he fell back on his talent for falsification of facts and documents. As proof of Clarke's perfidy, he produced a recording purporting to be a conversation between Clarke and a third party plotting to oust Hubbard from the partnership. When he played it back for Hubbard at home, the already tense Hubbard exploded. He rushed to his office and accused his partner of double-crossing him. Clarke vehemently denied everything, but Costa had done his work well. Hubbard was convinced that his partner had the ax out for him.

Quarreling, mutually suspicious partners are never good for business. Within a few months the once-thriving firm of Clarke and Hubbard was in trouble. After heated arguments and loud recriminations, the partnership was finally dissolved.

Hubbard tried to make a go of it alone, but his frazzled nerves gave him no peace. He could not concentrate. He lost his ability to forecast market trends. He no longer had even the patience to read stock tables. He would stay away from the office for days at a time. Finally he asked Costa's help.

Costa was glad to move a desk into Hubbard's office. And since Mrs. Hubbard had such good business sense and was an old hand at office routine, he suggested that she, too, help in reorganizing the business. It was a pleasant association and they worked hard and well together. The downward momentum, however, was not easily reversed. In the end, Hubbard was forced into bankruptcy.

The Costa plan was proceeding apace. Wrecking Hubbard's business had been comparatively simple. Wrecking the Hubbard marriage was going to be a lot harder and more complicated, but Costa was a determined man. Moreover, he enjoyed destroying people. His sadistic drive had not changed with his aliases. The compulsive malice with which he had railroaded Joseph Cohen to within minutes of the electric chair, his bitter crusade against Hearst, and his callous manipulation of Hans Schmidt were all instances of his monstrous capacity for evil for the sheer joy of doing evil. He had got no tangible advantage from any of these acts.

Hubbard, on the other hand, had something Costa wanted: Carol. The flame of conjugal love was undoubtedly burning somewhat less fiercely after almost ten years of marriage, but there was no doubt that Carol was still very much attached to Hubbard. Breaking that attachment would require skill and patience, but Costa had both. He was prepared to wait. He would even drive the high-strung Hubbard crazy if need be. Meanwhile he would give him a sharp jab with the poison pen.

For years the Hubbards had been very close to a Brooklyn family whose attractive young daughter sang in a church choir with Carol. One day the girl's father received an anonymous letter warning him that his daughter was having a clandestine affair with Edward Hubbard. The reason Hubbard lost his business, the letter explained, was that he was spending extravagant sums of money on the young choir singer. Although her father did his best to keep the shameful details of the letter secret, at least until he had had a chance to determine their validity within the family council, the gist of the letter somehow gained circulation in Brooklyn, and friends and neighbors of both families were soon buzzing with the supposed scandal.

Inevitably, the gossip reached the shocked ears of Carol Hubbard. And while the young choir singer was able to convince her parents that the story was a malicious lie, Carol wasn't so sure. After all, Hubbard had indeed been acting queerly of late, and perhaps the guilty secret of his liaison was responsible for his highly nervous state. Carol was ready to forgive him, but Hubbard did not want to be forgiven—he wanted to be believed. How could Carol not possibly see that the whole thing was a monstrous hoax, a lie, a diabolic plot to blacken his character? Very well, Carol agreed, she would accept his denial, but the coolness with which she made peace indicated that more than a little suspicion still remained.

This personal drama on top of his business failure was too much for Hubbard. He could not sleep at night. He was given to fits of weeping. He did not respond to the sedatives his doctor prescribed. He finally agreed to follow his doctor's advice and go away for a rest and change of scene. He retired to a small farm owned by an uncle in upstate New York. During his absence Costa saw quite a bit of Carol, but as a solicitous friend of the family, anxious about Hubbard's health, always ready to be of service to his absent friend's worried wife.

After four months Hubbard returned to the city, somewhat rested but far from robust. Carol had written to him regularly during his absence and welcomed him home with concern and affection. There was, however, an obvious change in their relationship that did not escape Costa, who was a frequent visitor. Costa did not fail to express concern for Hubbard's health. He never missed a chance to refer to the unfortunate collapse of the brokerage firm of Clarke and Hubbard and to try to analyze the cause.

Hubbard's nervous condition did not improve. In fact, his dejection slipped dangerously close to melancholia. His family physician was worried. When an old friend invited him to come out to visit him in Arizona—the friend lived in a small mining town—the doctor urged him to accept. Both

Carol and Costa agreed with the doctor. Convinced that the change might help him, Hubbard took off for the West—for a long stay.

When after six months Hubbard did not return, Costa began to show his hand—cautiously, but romantically. For the first time he told Carol he loved her. He did not tell her that Hubbard was a no-good; he merely said he was sorry he had not met her first, for she had married a man who was, while a fine person fundamentally, her inferior in intellect, charm, and the social graces. It is quite possible that Carol was the only true love of Costa's life, for he did not try to force the issue, to sweep her off her feet. He respected her puritan background, her innate decency, and her loyalty to Edward Hubbard. There was no doubt that she had begun to feel the irresistible hypnotism of the Musica-Johnson-Costa personality. Who, except Senator Reed, Ferdinand Pecora, and Jonah Goldstein, had seen through the golden aura of charm and overpowering poise that had veiled the chrysalis of the larva from Mulberry Bend? But Carol, the policeman's daughter, had a code of honor. She was not going to hit a man when he was down. She was not going to desert her husband of ten years because he was in financial and perhaps mental trouble. She appreciated Frank Costa's attentions and his sentiments, but. . . .

Musica-Johnson-Costa was not discouraged, not even when Ed Hubbard came out of the West ten months later, looking, talking, and acting like a new man. Hubbard was tanned, he was relaxed, and he was self-confident for the first time in years. He was grateful to Costa for his friendly concern for Carol during his long, enforced health furlough. And he was enthusiastically anticipating a second honeymoon with his wife. He was very happy.

6 : F. Donald Coster, M.D.

LATE IN 1923, Girard & Co., a small manufacturer of pharmaceuticals, opened its doors in a modest two-story building at 209 North Washington Avenue, Mount Vernon, New York. The firm produced *eau de quinine,* bay rum, hair tonics, colognes, and a furniture polish called Woodtone. Girard & Co.'s output, like that of Adelphi Pharmaceutical, was extremely high in alcohol content. Girard's plant, however, was far more imposing than the shabby set-up of the Brooklyn establishment, as was befitting the opulence, verdure, and dignity of the Westchester County environment.

The company was owned by F. Donald Coster, George Dietrich, and P. Horace Girard. Girard, for whom the company was named, was identified as a wealthy elderly uncle of F. Donald Coster, the active head of the firm. George Dietrich, actually the bookkeeper, was listed as treasurer. Other employees included Robert Dietrich, brother of George, and Dr. Emil Fanto, a Viennese chemist with a Heidelberg degree.

Out of the unsavory debris of his shattered, sordid past, Philip Musica had created a masterpiece of masquerade—Dr.

F. Donald Coster, native of Washington, D.C., alumnus of the University of Heidelberg (Ph.D., M.D.), President of Girard & Co., manufacturing chemists. For his new personality he could thank certain catalytic agents: the lifelong gleanings of an incredibly retentive mind, and the marked Thespian ability to lose himself in whatever character he chose. His definitive character was a superior creature completely equipped to compete in the uppermost strata of American social and economic life. Every trace of Mulberry Bend, Elmira, and the Tombs had been eradicated. Dr. F. Donald Coster was a sophisticated, intelligent professional man who quickly won the respect and admiration of Mount Vernon's leading citizens.

Dr. Coster felt so secure in his new impersonation that he brought his family back into the picture. Not that he had ever deserted them in his early post-Tomb days; his tribal instincts were too deeply ingrained for that. He had contributed generously to the support of his brothers and sisters, and after Mama Assunta came back from Naples with Robert and the two younger girls, he dined regularly with her to savor her homemade ravioli, her ossi buchi, and her baccalà with polenta. He had engaged in his familial activities discreetly, however, so as not to compromise his master plan. Now that he had molded his ultimate personality to his taste, he cast his brothers in new roles to fit his remodeled family tree.

The change of his own name from Frank D. Costa to F. Donald Coster was obviously a shift in emphasis from the Latin to the Germanic in line with his imaginary degrees from Heidelberg. Similarly, he rechristened his two younger brothers. George and Robert Musica became George and Robert Dietrich. The script called for Arthur, the oldest of his brothers, to play a part in which his family connection had to be concealed. Arthur, therefore, became George Vernard with apparently no direct connection with Girard & Co. The fictitious P. Horace Girard was part of the new genealogy Dr. Coster was working up for Mama Assunta.

Girard & Co.'s most valuable asset was a permit to withdraw 5200 gallons of alcohol a month. Formulas for the firm's products called for an unusually high alcoholic content, in some cases up to 90 percent. This made the merchandise extremely attractive to bootleggers and the profits of Girard & Co. spectacularly high.

Just how much of the thriving little company's business was legitimate was hard to determine even by contemporary records. There was enough bona fide trade to cover illicit sales and to satisfy the Volstead agents who checked the firm's operations regularly. Some of the Girard specialties were of high enough quality to compete in the established drug market, attracting customers that included leading department stores, retail drug chains, and large distributors of pharmaceuticals, among them McKesson & Robbins. There is little doubt, however, that most of the output found its way into bootleg channels.

While the illicit transactions were entered on the books at less than half the sums actually collected, they still reflected a creditable volume and the Girard balance sheets showed increasing profits. The firm had not been in operation very long before its expanded business justified an increase of some 400 percent in its withdrawal permit, allowing them 25,000 gallons a month—all verifiable by the Volstead agents. Under Dr. Coster's direction, George Dietrich made sure that the company's accounts could withstand the most rigorous inspection. On the books, the legitimate customers were recorded as the purchasers of the entire output. And

since Robert Dietrich was in charge of the shipping department, these records, too, were under big brother's watchful
control. And one of Girard's biggest customers was W. W.
Smith & Co., a sales agency headed by a man who called himself George Vernard, the oldest of the little brothers.

When the application for the startling increase in Girard
& Co.'s alcohol-withdrawal permit was submitted, Chief Federal Inspector Michael A. Silverstein was sent to Mount Vernon to check its validity. Any increase of that size was suspect.
and there had also been rumors about the firm's underground connections. The good doctor from Mulberry Bend
expected the inquiry and was ready for it. His records were
impeccable.

The volume of Girard's business with front-rank firms of
unquestionable integrity was sufficient to conceal its large
sales to customers of doubtful repute—which never appeared
on the records. Illicit sales were concealed by two methods.
First, they were falsely spread throughout the records of sales
to respectable firms, all supported by orders and invoices
carrying the names of the better department stores and other
enterprises beyond the suspicion of any federal inspector.
Second, the large sales volume attributed to W. W. Smith &
Co. took care of any other questions.

Actually it was through the Smith account that the main-
stream of the alcoholic products was diverted to the underworld. Years later George Dietrich (*né* Musica) revealed that
Girard & Co. sold *eau de quinine* and *lilas végétal* in quantities up to three-hundred-barrel lots, which skilled craftsmen
converted into "eight-year-old rye," "bottled-in-bond bour-
bon," and "Scotch" just off the boat.

During its first year of operation, Girard & Co. did almost
a half-million dollars of business. Government inspectors

had checked its honesty. For further expansion—a necessary step in the Coster timetable—the Girard company must be recognized in financial circles as a sound enterprise with great growth possibilities. Dr. Coster's nomination for proving this premise was nothing less than Price, Waterhouse, which he had heard described as the "blue ribbon outside auditors in the country." If such an outstanding firm could give its cold fish-eyed approval of Girard & Co., its prestige was assured.

In December of 1924, when the Girard company had been in business (and Dr. F. Donald Coster in existence) for little more than a year, Price, Waterhouse received a letter signed "P. Horace Girard," requesting a quotation for auditing the company's books on an annual basis. The letter also stated that the firm wanted advice on the installation of a new book-keeping system. "We expect to branch out in a different field during the coming year," wrote dear old nonexistent Uncle Horace Girard, "and we believe that our present system of bookkeeping could be greatly improved."

Girard & Co. became an account of Price, Waterhouse early in 1925. The fee for the first audit as of December 31, 1924, was $550, probably the greatest bargain Dr. Coster ever drove in all his driving existence. The Price, Waterhouse balance sheet was a prize exhibit attesting to the integrity and financial health of Girard & Co.

Dr. Coster, from his experience in the Great Hair Hoax, knew how auditors functioned, that they were interested in account books and supporting documents. He knew that they relied principally on figures entered in books and on papers of transactions, and that assets were verified only insofar as the figures were consistent. Accounts receivable, an important item, were checked by sampling records of selected customers' purchases, such as order slips, shipping records, duplicate invoices, and other bookkeeping evidences of sale. Inventories were checked only as to form, from tally sheets and records of product traffic. An auditor could hardly go into all the warehouses and check the merchandise item by item. Even if he had expert knowledge of the price and quantity of the tremendous variety of products controlled by accountancy methods, the cost of a physical audit of inventory would be prohibitive.

Price, Waterhouse certified that on December 31, 1924, Girard & Co. had assets of $295,000. This could hardly mean that the auditors had traced down all of Girard's customers or that they had done a companion audit of W. W. Smith & Co., which was responsible for more than 10 percent of accounts receivable. There was no reason for Price, Waterhouse to be suspicious. After all, during the last nine months of 1924, the Girard company had shown a $33,300 profit on sales of more than a quarter-million dollars. These figures were inflated, as were the inventory and accounts-receivable figures included in the claimed assets of nearly $300,000. But these figures, neatly marshaled under a Price, Waterhouse letterhead, were to Coster negotiable assets.

Dr. Coster was preparing to move in an expanded orbit. He would need financing. The small Mount Vernon bank that already looked upon Girard as a favored account suggested to Coster that he get in touch with Bond & Goodwin, a major investment banking house in New York. Bond & Goodwin sent one of their bright young men to Westchester to interview the potential client.

The Bond & Goodwin man who came to Mount Vernon to look into the affairs of Girard & Co. was everything that Philip Musica had wanted to be and that Dr. F. Donald Coster thought he had achieved. His name was Julian F. Thompson, Princeton '11, a sensitive, intelligent, perceptive man of sound social and financial background. He was impressed by the Price, Waterhouse balance sheet and by its list of highly regarded concerns with which the Girard company did business. He was even more impressed with Dr. F. Donald Coster, M.D., Ph.D. Coster was at his best as a charming, knowledgeable, intuitive, and efficient man of the world and man of affairs.

No two men could have been more different. Thompson, tall, thin, with a pince-nez balanced on the bridge of his long aquiline nose, had the reserved appearance of a scholar. Coster, his stocky figure boosted to five feet eight inches by elevator shoes, his round face and owl-like eyes behind heavy horn-rimmed glasses, was the paunchy, aggressive factory executive. Despite the difference in their looks and their fundamental beings, the two men were quickly in rapport. F. Donald Coster, the complete charlatan, faced a vital challenge to his chameleonic talents, but he had an advantage over Thompson. After all, the Ivy League aesthete had come only to evaluate the assets and character of a businessman, and to judge him as a financial risk.

Julian F. Thompson had never in his life encountered anything like this hybrid who had all the hallmarks of a thoroughbred. This Princeton alumnus, scion of a fine family who had spent his life among the socially acceptable and economically sound, had never been deceived by a counterfeit. He had always been able to spot the most gifted society impostor trying to crash the stag line at a top-drawer debut, and he had never yet been duped by a business mountebank.

Dr. F. Donald Coster fooled him on all counts. Thompson was captivated by Coster's charm, lulled by his apparent erudition, and moved to admiration by his grasp of his own business. He was not, however, hypnotized by the Girard company's figures. After scanning the books and studying the balance sheet, he told Coster that while the growth rate of the new company was impressive, it was still too small for Wall Street.

Coster agreed that Thompson's evaluation might be true for the present, but he outlined future plans that sent his new friend back to Wall Street with copious notes and unlimited enthusiasm.

As a gesture of friendship and with an optimistic eye on the potential of Girard & Co., Thompson wrote a brilliant seventeen-page brochure promoting the possibilities of the new firm. The brochure was a tipoff to the fact that while the Princeton man's vocation was investment banking, his avocation was writing. He demonstrated his talent as a playwright a few years later with *The Warrior's Husband,* a Broadway hit that launched Katharine Hepburn on her way to stardom. Thompson little realized that his Girard & Co. brochure was the prologue to a real-life drama starring the spurious Dr. F. Donald Coster, with himself cast in a tragic supporting role.

Coster added the prestige of Thompson's glowing panegyric to the distinction of the Price, Waterhouse audit and the asset of his alcohol-withdrawal (now grown fivefold) permit. This portfolio equipped him for his next move. Westchester had been a world away from Brooklyn. Fairfield County, the Gold Coast of Connecticut, was even more remote from the ghosts of his past. He acquired larger quarters in the abandoned plant of the Hawthorne Manufacturing Company on Waldemere Avenue in the town of Fairfield, halfway between the New York exurbanite bedroom of Westport and the bustling industrial city of Bridgeport.

Coster quickly made his presence known in the right places. He purchased his building through the agency of one local bank. He made respectable deposits in other Connecticut banks. He attracted the attention of business and civic leaders in the area.

One of the first men to fall under Coster's spell was Clinton Barnum Seeley, president of the Bridgeport-City Trust Company. Seeley was the grandson of Phineas Taylor Barnum, the fabulous showman. P. T. Barnum had been not only impressario of Jenny Lind, founder of sensational museums, and creator of the Barnum and Bailey circus but also mayor of Bridgeport; and his grandson retained a strong civic interest in the city. Apparently Clinton Barnum Seeley was not familiar with his grandfather's classic work *The Humbugs of the World.* Nor had he inherited the old showman's cynicism that gave tongue to the classic phrase, "There's a sucker born every minute." Grandpa Barnum must have been spinning dizzily in his grave as Seeley was succumbing to the blandishments of F. Donald Coster.

Seeley became so enthusiastic about Coster's prospects that he persuaded two other top officers of his Bridgeport bank to join him in an investment in Girard & Co. Seeley put up $20,-000; Egbert Marsh, a director of the bank, put up $6,000; and Horace B. Merwin, who later succeeded Seeley as president of the bank, came in for $2,000. This personal vote of financial confidence was given to Coster when he had been in the area only a month. Three months later, in May, 1925, the Bridgeport-City Trust Company lent Coster $80,000, which he repaid by the end of the year.

Girard & Co. continued to expand, and Coster needed more and more capital. In mid-1926 he approached the Bridgeport bank for a loan of $300,000. As this was a larger credit than Seeley's bank ordinarily handled alone, he and his associates enlisted the aid of R. F. Griggs & Co., investment bankers of Waterbury, Connecticut. Griggs arranged to raise the money by selling preferred stock in Girard & Co. to the Connecticut public. In less than a year and a half, Coster had won for himself a fervent clique of dewey-eyed sponsors and through them had acquired more than $400,000 of new capital.

Coster's quick and easy assumption of leadership among his new colleagues was done without conscious effort. Some quality inherent in him set him apart and above his fellows. Even as a youth his guidance was expected and accepted by his family and friends. The bankers and businessmen of Fairfield County, Connecticut, were no different from the sycophants of Mulberry Bend.

He regarded their adulation his just due as a great talent and a self-made aristocrat. Actually he was more than an aristocrat; he was an autocrat. He took no stock in the tenet *noblesse oblige.* He took the others into his retinue and permitted them to contribute capital, contacts, and prestige, while he created ideas and set policy. As a reward he gave them profits in such gratifying ratio to their investments that they were too dazzled to be curious. They had discovered a singular genius, and their faith in him was faith in themselves. They clasped him to their bosoms and invited him to join their most exclusive clubs.

Graciously aloof, he accepted their kudos and their sponsorship, but he walked alone.

7 : Benedict and Connecticut Squire

For all his whirlwind courtship of Connecticut high finance and exurban high society, Dr. Coster did not for a moment lose sight of the great love of his life. After all, he had destroyed a man to clear the way for his own wooing of Carol Jenkins Hubbard. He had betrayed the trust of a friend, wiped out his economic and social status, wrecked his self-confidence, maimed him in mind if not body. Yet for all the despicable, cold-blooded scheming with which the boy from Mulberry Bend had eliminated Ed Hubbard from Carol's life, his attitude toward Carol was unbelievably sentimental—pure, nineteenth-century romanticism.

He did not rush in immediately to claim his prize the moment Carol had divorced Hubbard; that would have given away the game. There is every reason to believe that Carol was not a party to Costa-Coster's machinations and that she was entirely ignorant of his cruel double-dealing. She was basically a decent person. She had refused to desert Hubbard when he was down in his luck. It was only after Costa-Coster's stratagems had made Hubbard appear dishonest that she made up her mind to leave him.

She may not have been ignorant of Coster's past. After all, she was already married to Hubbard when he was vainly trying to trace the Musica plunder in the hair swindle. And of course she had known Musica as a close friend during his Frank Costa period. It seems obvious at this distance that Carol Jenkins Hubbard's view of the man she knew as Frank Costa was the same as that of her then-husband and other men of good will who had gone through the same checkered period with him: a brilliant, underprivileged lad who had made two bad mistakes but who had demonstrated to the world that he had learned his lesson, paid his debt to society, and asked only that he be allowed to prove himself as a useful citizen.

After the collapse of her marriage, Carol had withdrawn to Long Island where she lived in seclusion among friends of her family. She was appreciative of Costa's discreet attentions, of his great consideration. And if she was any more immune to the hypnotism of his great charm than were the money men of Wall Street and New England, she would have been a superwoman.

Impatient as he must have been, Dr. Coster would not gather his romantic ideal to his couch and to his heart of hearts until he had prepared an enchanted castle worthy of receiving his Princess Charming. He spent most of 1925 putting down roots in Fairfield County (and making sure they would come up in golden blooms). A few days before the end of the year, however—December 29, 1925, is the date on the deed—he purchased the home that would provide the appropriately lavish environment for his long-dreamed-of and long-deferred marriage to the one woman in his life.

His purchase was a magnificent eighteen-room mansion at 400 Mill Plain Road in Fairfield. Standing on a seven-acre estate, the imposing edifice might have been a Florentine villa had it been built in Italy instead of Connecticut. It had once belonged to J. W. Hill, one-time publisher of the Bridgeport *Post,* the leading newspaper in that corner of Connecticut. But the tastes of a Heidelberg-educated genius could not be expected to coincide with those of the publisher of a provincial American newspaper. So Coster spent months and a small fortune tearing the guts out of the Hill villa, remodeling and redecorating.

One of his first purchases was a life-size photographic portrait of Theodore Roosevelt, which he hung in the library of his new home. He stocked the shelves of the library with an impressive selection of volumes dealing with medicine, chemistry, and economics. There were also a few scattered religious titles, none of which reflected the Roman Catholic upbringing of a boy who had escaped from Little Italy.

Although most of the villa was furnished in ponderous, unimaginative bourgeois style, Coster had gone out of his way to give a cosmopolitan air to the second floor. Here he had created an Oriental room, hung with Chinese paintings on silk, original Hiroshiges and Utamaros, ornamented with ivory and jade carvings, bronze Buddhas, cloisonné urns and sandalwood screens. Divans piled high with varicolored pillows gave the room the appearance of an Oriental potentate's zenana.

Also on the second floor was a large sunroom in which water gurgled from a fieldstone fountain, and rock gardens brightened the interior with exotic flora that were changed with the seasons.

The basement was remodeled for large-scale hospitality.

The recreation area was furnished with tables of all sizes, which seated twosomes to parties of ten, capable of serving a hundred guests. The handsome taproom had a twenty-foot mahogany bar with stainless-steel fittings. A wine cellar with automatic temperature controls was stocked with the finest wines and spirits—not the rotgut sold by the sleazy men who had made Coster rich, but genuine bottles obtained through influence, charm, or bribery. He stocked pre-Prohibition American ryes and bourbons, available only on physicians' prescriptions. His Scotch came in under diplomatic immunity. So did the wines, except those he wheedled from millionaires' cellars laid down before the Volstead Act. To match his fictitious German background, he made a great show of his Rhine wines and Moselles—vintage Bernkastler Doktor, Piesporter Goldtröpfchen, estate-bottled Diedesheimers and Hochheimers.

Coster's favorite corner of the basement was the poolroom in which a slot machine had been installed. He would spend hours feeding coins to the one-armed bandit, apparently trying to outwit a swindler of his own creation, since he himself could set the payoff combinations.

When in his opinion, the Connecticut palace was fit to receive his bride, Coster finally married Carol Jenkins Hubbard, the girl of his dreams. The date was May 1, 1926; the place, the First Reformed Church of Jamaica, Long Island. The Reverend Robert K. Wicht officiated and the attendants were David L. Hardenbrooke, a Queens real estate man, and Agnes Krause, both friends of the bride.

Coster the impostor could not help falsifying his marriage certificate somewhat. On it he identified himself as a chemist from New York City living on 150th Street, Jamaica, Long Island, with no mention of the Italianate castle in Connecticut he had prepared to receive his long-cherished bride. And he listed his parents as Anthony and Assumption (Girard) Coster, both born in the United States!

The Coster marriage license indicated that he was in full process of experimenting with his biographical background but had not yet found the pattern to suit him. In 1935, a birth certificate filed in Washington, D.C. (which he had decided should be his birthplace), again named his father as Anthony but rechristened his mother as Marie. A year later, in the form he submitted for listing in *Who's Who in America,* he had decided that his parents should be "Frank Donald and Marie (Girard) Coster." In the *Who's Who* biographical sketch he also pushed his marriage back five years to 1921, two years before Carol had divorced Hubbard. He was obviously trying to obliterate the name and face of Hubbard from his life. He also changed his wife's maiden name from Jenkins to Schieffelin, her mother's maiden name. This last revision was apparently an effort to connect Carol Jenkins with the socially prominent Schieffelin family, leaders for generations in the American pharmaceutical field.

When Coster's magnificent masquerade finally blew up with a loud noise and an overpowering odor, the red-faced editors of *Who's Who* spared no money or effort trying to find out how they could possibly have been duped into aiding and abetting an impostor. Their embarrassed answer was no more satisfactory than that of dozens of other victims: they had all been charmed silly by a consummate charlatan.

The *Who's Who* investigation did throw some light on the origin of Coster's fictitious family tree, however. The shame-faced researchers unearthed a volume published in 1846 under the unwieldy title *The Wealth and Biography of the Wealthy Citizens of New York,* listing alphabetically the most prominent capitalists of the period. On page 8 of this book, three Costers were listed: John Girard Coster, the father, and his sons John H. Coster and Girard H. Coster. The total Coster wealth was recorded at approximately $1,000,000, not exactly peanuts except when compared to the fortune of the No. 1 biographee of the volume, John Jacob Astor, whose net worth was estimated at $25,000,000.

The Costers were pre-Revolution settlers who came to New York from Holland, and were described in the 1846 tome as "gentlemen born and of irreproachable integrity." Also listed in the same volume of early New York capitalists was a Schieffelin family, apparently as appealing to Philip Musica as the Girards and the Costers when he began tailoring his and his wife's genealogy to match the pride of Fairfield, one of the oldest towns in Connecticut.

Had Musica bothered to delve a little deeper into family histories, he might have found something prophetic in the biography of another Coster, one Charles, a leading financier and partner in the Wall Street brokerage house of Coster, Knapp & Co. Charles Coster defrauded his customers of $2,000,000 and committed suicide when his misdeeds caught up with him.

Carol Jenkins Hubbard (Schieffelin) Coster took over as mistress of the Fairfield manor with a minimum of ceremony. She seemed to agree with her husband in discouraging the attentions of their neighbors and her husband's business as-sociates. She was much more interested in her hobby of raising chow dogs than in being introduced to Connecticut society. Her first alterations in the baronial Fairfield estate were to construct kennels and extensive dog runs in the rear of the chateau. The canine population was at times as numerous as thirty.

Coster shared his bride's love of pets. While he was not as chow-minded as Carol, he did on occasion allow himself to be photographed with his wife's champions. His own favorites were a huge Saint Bernard named Oscar and a foul-mouthed parrot who answered (profanely) to the name of Rickey. There were also a sheep who roamed the lawns and whole schools of tropical and other rainbow-hued exotic fish which flashed and glittered in spotlighted aquariums throughout the villa.

The Costers were to all appearances a pair of loving and animal-loving newlyweds.

While Dr. Coster's honeymoon went on and on in apparent perfect harmony, lovers' quarrels began to mar Coster's honeymoon with his Connecticut backers. His banker friends were, of course, in complete ignorance of the fact that the real growth of Girard & Co. was based on bulk sales of products with a high alcoholic content. Yet a firm could hardly become the largest source of alcohol for bootleggers in the Eastern states without some talk filtering back. Inevitably the rumors that Girard & Co. was engaged in illicit operations reached the ears of the bankers. Horace Merwin of the Bridgeport-City Trust was the first to mention the persistent gossip to Coster. Merwin later recalled that Coster became extremely indignant "and convinced me that everything was fine."

Officers of R. F. Griggs & Co., the Waterbury investment bankers that floated the Girard stock issue, also became perturbed by the rumors. Rowley W. Phillips, one of the Griggs officers, said afterward: "Naturally we traced down everything we heard. To the best of our knowledge then, there was no bootlegging. In the light of developments, we may have been wrong, but at the time we were convinced that everything was legitimate."

Federal agents agreed with the bankers. On several occasions Prohibition inspectors checked the Girard plant, but never took action. Coster charmed some of them and bribed others. His cover-up of sales was so ingenious that federal men who could not be convinced in any other way reluctantly agreed that there was no evidence of skulduggery.

His bold demeanor with the government people was enough to allay the suspicions of his associates. Some of them, perhaps, had no desire to delve too deeply. They loved the golden eggs of the miraculous Girard goose too much to risk stirring up a smelly omelet.

8 : Million-Dollar President

GIRARD & CO. was a half-million-dollar leap forward from the shabby (though prosperous) beginnings at Adelphi Pharmaceutical, but it was still on the ragged fringes of the great American drug industry. Ever since he had chosen pharmaceuticals as the shortest road to riches, Coster had been eying another Brooklyn firm as his ideal of stature and dignity in the trade. The prestigious concern had been operating at 55 Berry Street, Brooklyn, under the name of McKesson & Robbins.

McKesson & Robbins, then already almost a hundred years old, began its existence as the partnership of Olcott, McKesson & Co., which opened for business at 145 Maiden Lane, Manhattan, in 1833. The firm started as a drug wholesale house, but soon branched into manufacturing. On July 2, 1850, the firm of Olcott, McKesson was dissolved, and Daniel C. Robbins, a young pharmacist employed by the company, joined Charles M. Olcott and John McKesson in a partnership recorded as Olcott, McKesson & Robbins. When Olcott left the company in 1856, the firm name became McKesson & Robbins.

McKesson & Robbins grew with a growing nation. As the pioneers crossed the Mississippi and fanned out to the Pacific Coast, McKesson & Robbins was not far behind. Wherever clipper ship captains were stocking their sea chests with medicines for a long voyage, a McKesson & Robbins agent was at hand to offer them prime products. With the clipper ships, the reputation of McKesson & Robbins spread to the four corners of the earth, and with the covered wagons, to the new frontiers. The prestige of the firm in the newly won open spaces of the West is well established by a casual note in the old records of the company's history. An entry in an 1888 ledger notes the receipt of a bag of gold dust, worth $20,000, from a town in Montana. The covering letter read in part: "We want to open a drugstore out here. Send complete stock in return for the dust."

John McKesson represented the fourth generation of his family in America. His forebears had come from Scotland to found a distinguished colonial family. John had added enough acres to their early holdings to become one of the largest landowners and a leading citizen of Brooklyn. He had one son. His partner, Daniel Robbins, had two sons. The younger, Herbert, married a Carroll of Carrollton. The older, Dr. Charles A. Robbins, married a sister of Sara Delano and was therefore an uncle (by marriage) of Franklin Delano Roosevelt.

McKesson & Robbins became pioneers among American pharmaceutical manufacturers in the last decades of the nineteenth century. Dr. Robbins imported German pharmacists he had met at Heidelberg. They developed a quinine pill with a gelatin coating which made it a best seller in the humid climate of India. They were the first to produce a commercial hydrogen peroxide and compound stearate of zinc. McKesson & Robbins became one of the world's largest manufacturers of quinine and introduced other American botanical drugs into Europe and the Far East. (Quinine did not become a virtual East Indies monopoly until after the wily Dutch had introduced cinchona trees from Peru into Java.) The firm prospered and expanded. The five-story McKesson & Robbins building on Fulton Street was a New York landmark. The company printed its own labels and cut its own corks from Spanish and Portuguese bark. Forty salesmen represented the firm on the road and helped boost the annual income to $20,000,000.

Just before World War I, John McKesson, Jr., brought new blood into the company. John had been traveling in Europe with his wife when he met a big, personable man of considerable wealth who had retired from business and was devoting his time and talents to a study of cathedrals in France and Italy. The man's name was Saunders Norvell, and by a lucky coincidence, McKesson became greatly impressed by Norvell just as Norvell began to be bored by cathedrals. Norvell bought the shares of one of the partners in the drug firm and became chairman of the board with John McKesson, Jr., as president.

During the war years of 1914–18, the firm's prosperity reached new heights. However, competition was also moving ahead. E. R. Squibb & Sons, once a strictly scientific no-nonsense firm, had, since the death of old Dr. Squibb and the squabbles of his sons, passed into outside hands who believed in advertising, salesmanship, and toothpaste. Parke, Davis had made great progress in developing new botanicals. Merck and several other German firms had established manufacturing branches in the United States. All this cut into McKesson & Robbins' volume.

When John McKesson, Jr., died in 1924, control of the company was divided. The three McKesson sons—Irving, Donald, and George—inherited half of the shares, and Saunders Norvell and Herbert Robbins controlled the other half. The group was hopelessly divided on matters of policy. The McKesson brothers usually found themselves diametrically opposed to the views of Norvell and Robbins. The drug business was changing and the company's civil war was no help in adjusting to new conditions.

National distribution of McKesson & Robbins products had shrunk until it covered little more than the environs of New York City. The directors were split over the question of rebuilding a sales operation or abandoning it entirely in favor of outside distributors of the firm's products. A continued deadlock decided the two groups to sever relations. The McKesson brothers took over the manufacturing subsidiary The New York Quinine and Chemical Works, while Norvell and Robbins, assuming the corporate name, continued the wholesale drug business and special medicines line. The split came toward the end of 1924.

Operating as McKesson & Robbins at 55 Berry Street, Brooklyn, Saunders Norvell and Herbert Robbins continued to manufacture and sell milk of magnesia, cough syrup, quinine, and other family medicine-chest staples with a gross volume of some $5,000,000 a year. The distributing business, however, once the lifeblood of the firm, had dribbled away to almost nothing, so that shutting it down was a mere formality. Within two years, Saunders Norvell, who had made his fortune in hardware in the Midwest, was thoroughly disenchanted with the drug business. Robbins agreed with him that they would refuse no reasonable offer for the firm.

Almost overnight the word reached Dr. F. Donald Coster.

Coster had been preparing for just such an opportunity by systematically inflating the Girard assets. He now owned the firm by himself; P. Horace Girard, his imaginary partner and benevolent uncle, had conveniently died and left Coster his share of the stock. Coster's reputation as a gifted business-man was already such that the swift rise in Girard inventories and accounts receivable failed to disturb the auditors, the bankers, or the company officers. Coster was experimenting with the limitations of accountancy and the gullibility of financiers while they are making profits. Fresh capital con-tinued to flow in as he perfected the technique of expansion-through-fraud.

Early in the fall of 1926, Coster told his bankers that he could buy the old-line firm of McKesson & Robbins for $1,000,000. The enthusiastic response of his sponsors was another tribute to his peculiar genius. Completely seduced by his eloquent analysis of the tremendous potential of a merger with the venerable drug house, they leaped into ac-tion. A team of accountants checked McKesson & Robbins' books and assets. Two Connecticut investment banking firms —Bradley & Co. of New Haven and Fuller, Richter & Aldrich of Hartford—were invited to join the original underwriters. Supported by the Price, Waterhouse audits and the inspired testimonial of Julian Thompson, the bankers easily sold $1,650,000 worth of stock in a new firm—McKesson & Rob-bins of Connecticut.

Three years after his rebirth as Dr. F. Donald Coster, the boy from Mulberry Bend sat down at his desk, favored with a wise, owlish glance the fatuous sycophants he had hood-winked, and with a flourish signed a check for $1,000,000!

The date was November 11, 1926. Philip Musica was still under indictment for subornation of perjury. Although the indictment, handed up in January, 1921, was to be quietly quashed three years later, Coster on the day he signed the million-dollar check and became president of McKesson & Robbins of Connecticut was still a fugitive from justice.

This in no way prevented Dr. F. Donald Coster from immediately moving the operations of the respected old firm from Brooklyn into the plant of Girard & Co. in Fairfield.

As president of a million-dollar corporation, Coster did not forget his family. It was not altogether a matter of tribal loyalty. The further he advanced, the more he needed to protect his vulnerable rear. His key posts had to be manned by people he could trust. His brothers had proved reliable as Girard officers, so he moved them into comparable spots in the McKesson & Robbins organization: George Dietrich, his alter ego since the hair-importing debacle, came along as assistant treasurer (Coster shrewdly left the top treasurer's desk unoccupied for reasons of his own); Robert Dietrich, the youngest of the Musica boys, ran the shipping department. Arthur Musica, still using the name of George Vernard, continued to act as Coster's front man for his cover-up operations—W. W. Smith & Co., buying agent, and Manning & Co., Coster's private (and publicly unassociated) banking firm.

Coster also made sure that his new corporation would take care of Mama Assunta. When he set up a McKesson & Robbins office in downtown New York, he established it at 79 Cliff Street, a property that was owned, by curious coincidence, by Marie Girard, Mama Assunta's latest incarnation. The rental of $600 a month was collected for Mama through a real estate agent even after the corporation's offices were moved to Forty-fourth Street.

*   *   *

The expanded facilities of McKesson & Robbins strengthened the shield around the illicit alcoholic products that delighted the bootleggers. Years later George Dietrich was to testify that McKesson & Robbins' tincture of iodine was the product the underworld valued most highly. The spread between the boiling point of alcohol and that of iodine was so great that it was no trouble at all for bootleggers to distill off the lovely violet vapor of iodine before transforming the basic C_2H_5OH into "imported cognac," "Jamaica rum," and "premium Scotch." The bootleggers bought the tincture of iodine in fifty- or hundred-barrel lots. Much of the merchandise was channeled through the W. W. Smith company, which in turn saw that it went into highly respectable markets—on the W. W. Smith books.

Coster brazenly placed the names of the most reputable department stores on the customer lists of McKesson & Robbins. Some of the purchases were legitimate, some were the result of drug-department buyers being bribed or pressured into connivance. Invoices and other sales records were handled normally, but the merchandise was rarely delivered normally to the customer of record. It was picked up at the McKesson & Robbins platform by the bootleggers' trucks. In addition, there were two prices, one paid to McKesson & Robbins by legitimate customers for bona fide purchases; the other (roughly double) paid by the rotgut trade. The customer of record was also paid by the bootleg barons to show a slight profit on the "resale." The underworld trucks that, in the early stages of Coster's administration, picked up oceans of alcohol disguised as iodine, hair tonic, or mouth wash represented the most lucrative portion of McKesson & Robbins' business.

Coster's peculiarly acquisitive amorality resented having

to divide with his bankers these peculiarly personal profits. They were his, weren't they? He had invented them, and no one else knew about them, except the big-shot crooks who were professionally tongue-tied. These bankers were lesser creatures, unworthy of an equitable partnership in the rewards of this genius. Their smug acceptance of him as their peer irked him so that even in his most persuasive moments he would never treat them as equals. He charmed them with one hand and repulsed them with the other. They could be friendly, but never intimate. He would feather his nest with their own down, and they would not even know he had plucked it from them.

It was curiously typical of his dichotomous nature that while he was plotting to skim profits from the company's treasury for his own illicit gain, he was also fighting fiercely and valiantly for the fortunes and aggrandizement of Mc-Kesson & Robbins. His bustling business with tincture of iodine had brought him face to face with the monopolies controlling the international drug trade.

Iodine, for instance, came largely from South America as a by-product of the nitrate industry. To keep distribution and prices in profitable balance, a combination of a few American firms had exclusive access to the iodine obtained from the mother liquor during the purification of Chilean saltpeter. Coster sent a man to Chile to buy iodine from the same sources serving his competitors. After repeated failures, Coster's agent finally purchased a shipment financed by a letter of credit from the Bridgeport-City Trust Company.

No sooner had the ship bearing Coster's iodine left the port of Iquique, however, than the iodine trust reacted. Under pressure from the monopolists, the Chilean government seized the ship and returned it to dock. The infuriated

Coster took this as an insult and a personal challenge and gave immediate battle. He hired a former president of Chile to get his iodine back, and once the political wheels began turning, he refused to let them stop until he had broken the hold of the monopolists on the Chilean market. Thereafter, McKesson & Robbins could buy and ship iodine direct from Chile on the same terms as its competitors.

Having licked the iodine trust, Coster next went after the quinine monopoly. Until the middle of the last century, the world's quinine was made from bark grown in the Peruvian Andes and named after the wife of the Spanish viceroy to Peru, Countess Chinchón, whose malaria it cured in 1638. In 1852 the Dutch started experimenting with transplanting cinchona trees from the Peruvian Andes to tropical highlands in Java of about the same altitude and latitude. By the end of World War I, some 90 percent of the world's quinine came from Java, most of it from the great government factory in Bandung, and the market was made in Amsterdam. The American drug firms with the inside track in the Netherlands cold-shouldered every attempt by McKesson & Robbins to join the quinine club.

Each rebuff strengthened Coster's determination to break the monopoly. He finally hired a Bridgeport attorney named Jonathan Grout to represent him. Grout, a brother-in-law of Horace Merwin, who had become president of Bridgeport-City Trust, carried the fight into the equity courts. After a long battle Coster won out, and McKesson & Robbins was admitted to the inner circle of the lucrative quinine trade.

Coster then took on the monopolists who had tied up the Bolivian bismuth market—and won again.

His successful antitrust crusades were watched with deep interest by the whole drug industry. Trade journals particu-

larly gave wide publicity to his victories, and Coster won enthusiastic national acclaim as the wizard who single-handed
had defeated the powerful combines that nobody had dared
challenge before. His brilliant display of genius simplified
his next task. Convincing his happy sponsors that he was an
expert of experts in the field of international drug procure-
ment was child's play. He had discovered the device with
which to skim off the cream of McKesson & Robbins' profits
for his own use.

In October, 1927, Dr. F. Donald Coster organized McKesson & Robbins, Ltd., a Canadian corporation established for
the purpose of trading in crude drugs outside the United
States. The new corporation would be a totally owned subsidiary, and the same Connecticut financiers who had boosted
Dr. Coster to his present heights would be directors in the
Canadian firm. The business of buying and selling crude
drugs in foreign markets, however, would be Coster's private
preserve. How could it be otherwise? He had already demonstrated how the master hand could tame the overseas monopolists. His retentive mind had already been overactive in
the homework of titles, terminology, and the geography of
the crude drug trade.

Coster's eloquence, his apparent expertise on the sources
and nature of crude drugs, and his "personal acquaintance"
with nabobs in the exotic lands which furnished the nards,
the balsams, and the elixirs dazzled the Bridgeport bankers.
They were enchanted by the strange chemistry of the mysterious East, by the herbs and flowers, by the oils and gums,
the health-giving—and profit-producing—seeds and extracts.
They had no idea what he was talking about when he spoke
glibly of "balsam of Tolu, Borneo benzoin, storax and styrene
and cinnamic acid," but they trusted him implicitly. Had he

not already multiplied their original investments spectacularly? Would it not be short-sighted not to follow him in this new venture? As one of his backers remembered years later: "He had a way of inspiring awe as well as imagination. There was a strange aura of greatness about him."

At the end of 1927, Coster was able to show a profit of some $600,000 for McKesson & Robbins. This included "earnings" from the new crude-drug division. And, since Coster had learned from his Girard experience that auditors may be gullible souls who deal with figures rather than concrete realities, the amount also included fat listings of accounts receivable and a large reported inventory. The profit statement was enthusiastically received by the investors, a result which was, after all, Coster's objective.

He was now ready to move ahead to the next stage.

9 : The Course of Empire

COSTER was riding his destiny hard. In four years he had pyramided a few thousand dollars into a $4,000,-000 manufacturing concern with a century-old name. He had surrounded himself with backers and directors of impeccable social and economic standing, and he had been accepted as their equal. He had a wife whom he loved dearly, and her palace was the envy of many of his Connecticut neighbors who, a dozen years earlier, would certainly have considered themselves his betters. He had a million-dollar subsidiary in Canada, which was his private piggy bank. What was there now to keep him from his ultimate goal—Wall Street and the Big Board?

Wall Street had been his dream for sixteen years, from the time the United States Hair Company had had its brief flurry on the Curb Exchange. He hoped to make it with Girard & Co., but he had not quite cleared the hurdle of Bond & Goodwin in the person of Julian F. Thompson. But now, having resurrected McKesson & Robbins in little more than a year, and with another million-dollar corporation rising from the spoils of his victory over the international monopolists. . . .

Coster telephoned Julian Thompson, asking him to come to Fairfield to listen to future plans.

Thompson came at once. With the dramatist's pride of authorship, he felt that F. Donald Coster was a little bit his creation. He had discovered the genius in the obscure Girard laboratories in Mount Vernon, New York, and he had shared vicariously in his protégé's successive triumphs. Now Coster was offering him real participation in what seemed certain to be a master stroke.

Two vital elements in the American economy favored Coster's latest and most ambitious plans. One was the irresistible witchery of the stock market for the American public. Coster was aware that Wall Street was a mirage, a shimmering orchard of golden apples just waiting to drop into the laps of the first comer. In 1927 every Main Street in the country was crowded with people clutching handfuls of money that they wanted to invest. The second factor was a crisis in the American drug industry.

Thompson listened carefully, entranced as usual. When he heard the details of Coster's impressive project, he nodded and said: "At last you are big enough for Wall Street."

Coster's scheme was simple but breathtaking in its scope. It was nothing less than a blueprint for a three-way merger of wholesalers, jobbers, and retailers in the drug trade. Retail drugstore chains were spreading across the country, locating in the big cities with heavy traffic patterns and creating problems for the small-town druggist.

Individually owned drugstores were serviced by regional distributors, for the most part old-line family firms such as Langley & Michaels on the West Coast, Murray Drug Co.

in South Carolina, Fuller-Morrisson in Illinois, Hall-Van Gorder in Ohio, and Farrand, Williams & Clark in the Detroit area. These old established houses were highly regarded in their regions, but they were puny competition for the growing chains. The second- and third-generation heads of the family firms were disenchanted by the state of the once-lucrative business, and seemed unable to procure a varied enough line of products to meet modern needs. The picture was grim.

Coster, however, had just the brand of gilt to brighten things up. The heart of the matter was distribution, and Coster's plans would benefit not only the regional distributors and the retailers but also McKesson & Robbins—and F. Donald Coster. His plan called for a consolidation of the regional distributors (who would be provided with a complete line of McKesson & Robbins products) and allowed retailers also to join by taking stock in the parent company engineering the merger. The guiding hand, of course, would be Coster's.

Julian Thompson was so impressed by the project that he put his own reputation and the prestige of Bond & Goodwin behind it. He prodded bankers into backing the plan with financial support, and he himself crisscrossed the country in overnight sleeper jumps to sell the idea to the hinterland distributors. He was back in no time with the signatures of sixteen of them who were ready to consolidate under the aegis of McKesson & Robbins (read Coster).

In August, 1928, a new holding company was chartered: McKesson & Robbins, Incorporated (Maryland), combining the functions of McKesson & Robbins of Connecticut with those of the regional distributors Thompson and Coster had brought into the fold. Thompson was treasurer of the holding company and worked out the details of each transaction.

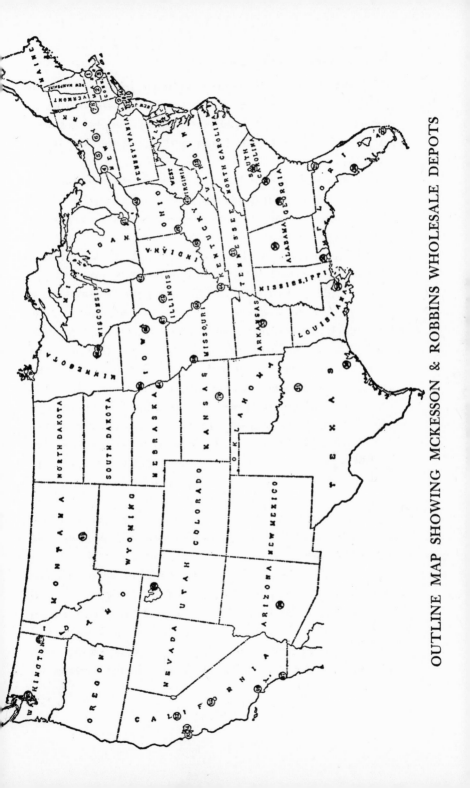

OUTLINE MAP SHOWING MCKESSON & ROBBINS WHOLESALE DEPOTS

The distributors were given cash and stock in the new corporation. The money was raised through a $9,700,000 issue of preferred stock sold by Bond & Goodwin, Goldman, Sachs, and, to a lesser degree, the Bridgeport and Waterbury bankers.

Through wholly owned subsidiaries, the parent company manufactured its own drugs and household remedies as well as distributed a varied line of specialties made by other firms. Other regional distributors soon joined the original sixteen, frightened by the growth of such giant chains as Liggett, Rexall, and Walgreen. The chains were crowding out the independent retailers on whom the regional firms depended, so the distributors welcomed the broader base from which they could compete. They were given local autonomy, plus the advantage of being able to supply their area customers with McKesson & Robbins drugs as well as the products of other member firms with centralized distribution.

Coster's first annual report to his stockholders, as of December 31, 1928, promised a strong cooperative relationship with the neighborhood druggists. He offered the retailers a plan for buying up to one hundred shares of McKesson & Robbins stock on time payments. He also offered stock to his employees both at home and in the field.

The first annual report boasted of economies achieved by elimination of duplication. In one operation, six men were doing the work formerly done by 62, thus saving $250,000 a year. Centralizing manufacturing activities under one roof at Bridgeport, Coster pointed out, avoided "duplication of expense and effort of a very large group of chemists, pharmacists, superintendents and foremen. Buying, credit, sales, and other important departments are being rapidly consolidated. These economies . . . should be reflected in 1929 earnings."

The annual report did not mention the fact that the consolidation and reorganization of administrative functions would give him complete personal control over the vast finances of a huge corporation.

The commodious recreation rooms in the villa on Mill Plain Road were almost deserted during the years that Coster was building his empire. The hundred-guest capacity of the basement party area was never used. Now and then Coster would invite two or three couples for supper and an hour or so of bridge. His entertaining was rather stiff and formal, and although he always offered cocktails and a bottle of wine, he himself rarely took more than a polite sip, never enough to unbend to the point of cordiality. He had to favor his ulcer, he explained.

Mrs. Coster was scarcely more of a social person. She seemed more interested in her chows than in her neighbors or the members of the Connecticut elite whose invitations her husband usually turned down without consulting her. She occasionally entertained her mother, Mrs. Carrie Jenkins, who came over from Queens now and then, and her two brothers, Leonard and John Jenkins. Her secondary interest, after her dogs, was spiritualism, and she often read books on the occult.

It was a good life on Mill Plain Road. There was no need for Carol to lift a finger to run her household. There were plenty of servants. Over the two-car garage (a Packard and a Lincoln) lived the gardener and his wife (who did the laundry). The chauffeur slept out. There was also a butler, a cook, and from one to two maids as the occasion demanded. Her closets bulged with expensive gowns. She had charge accounts at all the most fashionable stores of Fifth Avenue and Fifty-seventh Street, and her annual contribution to the economics of *haute couture* sometimes ran into five figures.

Coster's relations with his own family, the ex-Musicas, were privately closer than ever and publicly more and more ostentatiously distant. Mama Assunta had acquired a transplanted bit of Italian countryside on Long Island, a twelve-room mansion in the Roman manner not far from Westbury. Two of her daughters, Grace and Evelyn, lived with her. Lucy, the youngest of the girls, had died in 1920, and Louise, the oldest was now Mrs. Robert Guex, wife of the head gardener on the Hudson River estate of Henry Morgenthau, who was to be President Franklin Roosevelt's Secretary of the Treasury. Grace had adopted the same name Coster had given his mother, Marie Girard, and Evelyn had married a man named Calafato, who seems to have disappeared somewhere along the line. All three women were active in the affairs of St. Brigid's Church in Westbury and in community matters generally. Some Long Islanders still remember the two sisters for their old-fashioned manner of dress and for their charitable works. They distributed great quantities of medicines, certainly from McKesson & Robbins, to the ailing poor of the region.

Mama Assunta was remembered (as Mrs. Marie Girard) largely for her astounding proportions. She had always tended toward the spherical, and her long diet of pasta, polenta, and gnocchi had made her positively grotesque. She weighed closer to 300 than 200 pounds, quite a load for a woman less than five feet tall to carry around. Her obesity worried her doctor more than it did Mama Assunta. Dr. Stephen Petrovitz, who discussed her symptoms with her oldest son (and was stunned when he learned years later that the man so knowledgeable about medicine had never been near a medical school), found that she had a cardiac condition, diabetes, and an enlarged liver. She never lacked for pharmaceuticals.

Coster called his mother several times a week. Whenever he could make a secret excursion to Long Island, he hurried to Mama Assunta's for a family dinner. Here he could relax, shed his austere Teutonic mask, and let his hair down. While gorging himself on Mama's homemade manicotti and saltimbocca and basking in the Latin warmth of his family, he could really laugh with full-throated, belly-shaking Neapolitan glee. He would talk the language of his youth, for Mama Assunta had never quite mastered English. And when he kissed her good-by, it was with the satisfaction of knowing that he had at last made her dream come true.

His brothers George and Robert, the pseudo-Dietrichs, he never saw outside the office, although he had made them both into suburbanites. George drew $10,000 a year as assistant treasurer and dabbled in real estate on the side. He lived in a better than average house on Brookmere Drive, in a quiet residential part of Fairfield, with his blond outgoing wife, Claire, and their five children. Like his brother Robert, and Coster as well, George was a Mason, a Shriner, and a Republican.

Robert and his shy wife, Anne, lived with their two children in a modest home in the Stratfield section of Fairfield. Aside from his duties as head of the shipping department, Robert was a busy extrovert who was constantly engaged in some community activity. He organized and managed the McKesson & Robbins baseball team. If a fast, hard-hitting shortstop had trouble reading labels or operating a capsule machine, Robert would put him in some department where he could do no damage and on batting-practice days would punch his shortstop's time card himself. He was a determined joiner. At Christmas he would don a Santa Claus suit and distribute gifts to the homes of company employees.

Only brother Arthur, renamed George Vernard, remained outside the suburban circle. As Coster wanted to keep the operations of W. W. Smith & Company and the Manning bank in the background as much as possible, he insisted that Vernard live first in Manhattan, later in Brooklyn.

As McKesson & Robbins of Maryland gained amazing momentum, Coster moved his holding-company treasurer into the Connecticut orbit. While Brother Arthur was relegated to New York, Julian Thompson, distinguished Princetonian, still-unfulfilled writer, esthete, and Diogenes of Wall Street, was given an office in the Fairfield executive suite and urged to pull up his New York roots and become a suburbanite. After all, his reputation for integrity, his social standing, his acknowledged intelligence, and particularly his great and admiring faith in F. Donald Coster, M.D., Ph.D., were all qualities Coster wanted to have within thumb range.

Coster had plenty of valid arguments. The original sixteen regional drug distributors whom Thompson had enticed under the McKesson & Robbins umbrella had multiplied to sixty-six. In addition to the original authorized capitalization for the holding company of 5,000,000 shares of no-par common stock and 500,000 shares of $50 preferred, Coster was already aiming at a capitalization of $250,000,000. With Thompson's help, he would raise $22,000,000 by an issue of twenty-year debentures at 5½ percent. Common stock was already quoted at above the book value of preferred shares— a little better than $50—on the Big Board in Wall Street. To the new members of the merger, the old family firms that had watched their traditional profits slowly drying up until they acquired McKesson & Robbins stock, the smell of money was intoxicating. The Connecticut bankers too, although they might have become surfeited with the aroma, still found it attractive. Clinton Barnum Seeley's original $20,000 investment was by then worth more than a million. Even cynical old Grandpa P. T. Barnum would have been impressed.

Julian Thompson, who had been impressed for years, jumped at the chance of moving to the suburbs and sitting at the right hand of the genius he had helped discover. After all, he had not only personally enticed the regional distributors into joining the monumental Maryland holding corporation, but he had upheld Coster against early opposition to the merger plans from Horace Merwin and other Bridgeport bankers. Merwin had thought the plan too ambitious and suggested a trial project involving only a few New England companies. Again Coster had been right.

After the turmoil of Wall Street, Thompson found the comparative peace of the Connecticut countryside refreshing. Although he kept his Park Avenue apartment as a *pied-à-terre,* he bought the Twin Silo Farm on Catamount Road in Fairfield and settled his family in a fourteen-room house hidden away on 120 rolling acres. There were a brook and a small lake on the farm, but as there were also barns and dairy buildings, Thompson decided he would make a hobby of farming. He bought twenty-six head of prize cattle, some of them costing as much as $2,500 a head, invented and patented a special container, and sold milk under his own label. Before long, however, his hobby became a business and took too much time away from the growing affairs of McKesson & Robbins. He then became a supplier for the Mitchell Dairy, one of the largest milk distributors in Connecticut.

Thompson's office was in the executive suite on the second

floor of the McKesson & Robbins building in Fairfield. The plant was (and is) north of the Boston Post Road where Fairfield nudges the westerly fringes of Bridgeport. Coster's office was a large corner room flanked on one side by the directors room and on the other by George Dietrich, his alter ego who still bore the title of assistant treasurer. A file room staffed by three clerks separated Dietrich's office from that of his nominal superior, Treasurer Thompson, which was at the front of the administrative clerical staff area. Across the unpartitioned domain of the clerks and typists was the office of John H. McGloon, the company comptroller, and that of Lucretia Vanderbilt Cosmetics, a mail-order project for the sale of perfume and lipstick through coupon advertising in the women's magazines. Robert Dietrich, head of the shipping department, looked after the dimes and quarters that rolled in from the coupon clippers.

George Dietrich was not only the Cerberus of the executive suite, guarding Coster from unwelcome visitors, but he was also the only person besides Coster who regularly handled the affairs of McKesson & Robbins, Ltd., of Canada. On the rare occasions that George had to be away, brother Robert would sit in for him, thus keeping the business of the Canadian subsidiary a family matter—and with reason. For the business of McKesson & Robbins, Ltd., of Canada, was strictly funny business.

The Canadian firm did millions of dollars' worth of trading in crude drugs throughout the world—according to the records. Actually, no crude drugs ever changed hands. In one of the most intricate, ingenious, and well-organized frauds of all time, correspondence poured into Fairfield reporting purchases and sales in all parts of the globe. The crude drugs were being stockpiled in Canadian warehouses pending a favorable market, Coster reported, and evidence to that effect was presented to the auditors on letterheads of such firms as P. Pierson & Co., B. Miller & Co., H. D. Becker & Co., A. H. Raymond & Co., H. Monroe & Co., C. H. Williams & Co., and D. C. Reynolds & Co. The "profits" were phenomenal in inventories and accounts receivable. With the complicity of his dummy purchasing agent, W. W. Smith & Co., and the fictitious Manning bank, it was a simple matter for Coster to siphon off whatever money he needed for his personal use.

The clearing house for all mail transactions of the Canadian subsidiary was George Dietrich's office. A great dovecote of a mail rack filled one corner of the room and George's day began with his standing in front of the pigeonholes, opening all letters addressed to the administrative offices before rerouting them to the individual addressees. Even mail addressed to his nominal superior, Treasurer Julian Thompson, was opened by George. Thompson frequently complained to Coster of this invasion of privacy, but Coster always laughed it off. Humor him, he told Thompson. George is an impassioned philatelist. For as long as I've known him he has been a stamp collector, and he cannot resist all these beautiful foreign postage stamps that come in from crude-drug dealers all over the world. Humor him. . . .

There was nothing humorous about George Dietrich's privilege of writing checks for unlimited amounts or his ready access to the walk-in vault that often contained a fortune in cash. Julian Thompson did not mention either of these points, probably because at this stage of company history he was not aware of them.

Outside of the four Musica brothers, no one was aware of the blueprint by which the imaginary crude-drug division was supported by four pillars. The first prop was the network of mail drops that constituted the offices and warehouses of the far-flung fictitious corporation. Second was the inventory control, sufficiently credible to satisfy the expert auditors of Price, Waterhouse. Third was the checkbook and cash in George Dietrich's uncontrolled possession. And fourth was the two-headed family chimera—W. W. Smith & Co., international trading agents, and Manning & Co., private bank and fiscal agent for McKesson & Robbins.

And so the money rolled in.

10 : Big Wind on Wall Street

D URING the euphoric late 1920's, McKesson & Robbins, with Coster at the helm, literally flew before the brisk, gold-scented winds of Wall Street. The year 1929 opened optimistically. Paper millionaires born in the 1928 bull market were riding tall in the saddle and eating high on the hog. Members of the New York Stock Exchange had more than a half-million customers on their books dealing on margin, and a million more buying and selling for cash. It was the most frenetic gambling orgy in history. From Main Street to Fifth Avenue, in every city, town, and village, Americans were speculating on the stock market. In September, 1929, harried New York City brokers were in debt to the tune of $8,500,000,000 supporting the accounts of their customers. The wealth of the nation was being pumped up with the hot air of imaginary fortunes into a fantastic balloon straining to snap its inadequate overtaxed guy wires.

The Federal Reserve Board tried vainly to close a valve against the inflationary gush of borrowed money by increasing the rediscount rate and uttering grave warnings against the perils of the situation. The words were lost in the wildly enthusiastic roar of people who arose each morning confident that they would be millionaires by suppertime. What was the difference if one paid 6 percent or 10 percent for the chips if every hand in the game was a royal flush?

Dr. F. Donald Coster, who had always been a Wall Street buff, was in the merry game up to his eyebrows. He had accounts with several brokers under different names. He opened accounts in his wife's name and in the names of her two brothers, John and Leonard Jenkins. He even resurrected old P. Horace Girard, his "partner and uncle," who had quietly disappeared during the Girard & Co. period but who was now needed for stock-market purposes. His Connecticut colleagues were not in on Uncle Horace's "decease" while owner of the Mount Vernon firm, so they were not taken aback when Coster informed them sadly that the "wonderful old man" was dying of tuberculosis. To Merwin, the Bridgeport banker, and Phillips, of the Waterbury investment house, he confided that in appreciation of their help in promoting the Maryland holding company, he was going to let them in on a good thing. He explained that Horace Girard's estate included 20,000 shares of McKesson & Robbins stock. Since the firm's securities were relatively inactive, the dumping of such a large block of shares on the market would be catastrophic.

Girard knew he was dying, Coster said, and was worried about inheritance taxes, so he had little trouble in convincing the old man that he should sell the stock. If Merwin and Phillips wanted to join him in taking the stock off the old man's hands—Coster himself could handle only a small part —he was sure they could get concessions which would make the price attractive. The stock would have to be transferred privately, of course, since fluctuations in the market might affect the merger talks going on with still more companies on the verge of joining the McKesson & Robbins complex. If the stock went up, the stockholders might not approve the pending deals. If it went down, some of the wholesalers might have second thoughts about the mergers.

Merwin and Phillips were delighted. Since there was too much money involved for them to handle alone, they asked Coster's permission to invite some of their friends into the pool. When he acquiesced, they brought practically every important banker and industrialist of the region into the deal. In order to preserve the secret nature of the transaction, brokers were barred and principals were asked to deal with Coster on a personal basis and not through their respective companies. All checks were sent directly to Coster himself. His partners were happy and grateful, and he was richer by some $500,000.

Everyone concerned was properly sympathetic upon learning a short time later that P. Horace Girard had passed away. No one was aware that the stocks had been held in the name of Coster's sister Marie Girard (née Grace Musica) and not of P. Horace Girard, the phantom uncle.

While the stock market continued climbing to dizzier and dizzier heights, and the coast-to-coast program of consolidation was making rapid progress, mostly on stock and cash transfers, Coster ran into fresh trouble. The Federal Trade Commission hit McKesson & Robbins (Maryland) with a charge of violating the Clayton Antitrust Act. The new holding company, according to the complaint filed with the F.T.C., by acquiring the capital stock of twenty-eight wholesale drug firms in a number of states, had acted wilfully and illegally "to substantially lessen competition" and to create a monopoly in certain drugs and proprietary medicines.

Coster had done his political homework and was ready with an answer to the F.T.C. charges. He had previously submitted a statement of facts to the Justice Department, he explained, and had been assured that his plans for consolidation would meet no objection. He pointed out:

> McKesson & Robbins has brought under a single ownership a group of long-established drug houses in different parts of the country. This organization has made possible a comprehensive service to independent drug retailers and has been enthusiastically endorsed by retailers the country over.

The F.T.C. charges were quietly dropped.

The madness in Wall Street came to an end on Terrible Tuesday, the blackest day in the history of the New York Stock Exchange. On October 29, sixty-three days before the end of intoxicating 1929, Wall Street reaped the whirlwind which blew a $55,000,000,000 frosting off the American cake.

Faced with impending disaster, Coster used every maneuver his agile, devious mind could devise to keep McKesson & Robbins afloat. A newcomer to the Big Board, the firm was in a precarious position. Years later, George Dietrich testified that at the time of the crash Coster was worth $6,500,-000 and that most of his private fortune went into supporting McKesson & Robbins stock during the critical days. He was able to induce some of his more venturesome colleagues to take a similar gamble.

In the first three days following the market collapse, Coster dipped into the company treasury for $634,000 to cover margin demands on his own brokerage accounts. To do this he merely had George Dietrich send cashier's checks directly to George Vernard at W. W. Smith & Co. for what was ostensibly a transaction on behalf of the Canadian subsidiary. Coster must have had grave misgivings about using such brazen methods of larceny, for in 1932 the fraudulent operations of McKesson & Robbins of Canada became much smoother and outwardly proper.

In 1929, however, Coster's principal worry was the morale of his new subsidiary members, many of whom were now having doubts about the wisdom of consolidation. Having surrendered their independent status, some of them for stock alone, they were watching the stock market with fascinated horror. As the successive shocks of the crash reverberated, McKesson & Robbins' superstructure trembled with the rest. Coster kept it from toppling by driving himself, his associates, and the entire personnel of the company at an unmerciful pace. His capacity for work amazed his tense, frightened colleagues, increasing their respect and admiration into a kind of traumatic awe.

With the complete and unquestioned control of the company in his own hands, Coster succeeded in slowly stabilizing its position. It was a false stability, of course, based on fictitious inventories in nonexistent warehouses in Canada, on bogus accounts receivable, and mythical expansions. However, as nobody dreamed that the Canadian subsidiary was purely a figment of Coster's imagination, the millions of dollars in Canadian assets on the McKesson & Robbins balance sheet did much to see the firm through the desperate last weeks of 1929.

Coster was constantly incubating new ideas for meeting the succeeding crises. Some of the schemes were legitimate, all were ingenious. One typically Coster trick was to buy up stores of cheap drugs from bankrupt pharmaceutical firms and carry them on his own inventory at many times their actual value.

One smart piece of public relations he borrowed from the

Vick Chemical Company, which, on November 8, 1929, offered its customers in the retail trade the opportunity to cancel subscriptions for stock of the Vick's Financial Corporation, pledging to return money already paid in by those wishing to cancel. A few days later Coster called the financial desk of the New York *Times* from his Fairfield office to report a similar offer:

> Although no public announcement was made at the time immediately after the first crash two weeks ago, we offered to repurchase for cash on demand all McKesson & Robbins rights held by retail druggists. We also offered to cancel McKesson & Robbins subscriptions of retail druggists if desired. Very few requests for refunds on rights or subscriptions have been received. Our participation plan for retail druggists has not been withdrawn.

So successful was Coster's desire for personal anonymity while seeking publicity for his firm that the financial editors of the solid, old New York *Times* had apparently never heard of the president of McKesson & Robbins. When quoting Coster's statement, the *Times*, the fourth estate's meticulous model for accuracy, spelled his name "Koster."

The Coster statement did much to bolster confidence and prevent a selling wave which could have proved disastrous to the company. Many aspects of the final mergers were still months away and might have been adversely affected.

Another confidence builder, also legitimate, was the assurance of a twenty-five-year supply of cod liver oil. Coster arranged for McKesson & Robbins to take over the entire capital stock of a Norwegian firm known as Isdahl & Company A/S, and to make the firm's founder, J. C. Isdahl, a director of McKesson & Robbins (Maryland). Isdahl's company surrendered all assets except producing and refining plants, which were reorganized as Isdahl Eindomsselskab A/S, and contracted to sell its entire output of cod liver oil for twenty-five years to McKesson & Robbins' new Norwegian subsidiary.

Coster got Stock Exchange approval for the listing of additional shares—5,518 of common and 3,486 of convertible preferred—to be used in the Norwegian transaction. Permission was also granted to list a further 3,486 shares of common stock for the conversion of preferred stock used in the deal.

The grinding Depression that followed the stock-market crash eroded the foundations of every business enterprise in the nation. Bankruptcies ran into the thousands. Factories without customers shut down. Bread lines stretched from coast to coast, made up of people who were used to eating cake. Millions of families existed on the bare subsistence handouts of government agencies and private philanthropies. The street-corner apple seller became a symbol of the era.

McKesson & Robbins salesmen were not reduced to selling apples, yet despite its turnover of $140,000,000 in 1929, the Year of the Big Wind, and its false assets, the firm might have had trouble weathering the storm without the cash income from its illegal alcohol sales. The bootleggers' trucks still rolled up to the platform in Fairfield at night to load barrels of hair tonic, furniture polish, and tincture of iodine.

When the firm squeaked through the first Depression years without disaster, McKesson & Robbins executives began to breathe more easily. Some of them resumed their efforts, interrupted by the crash, to persuade Coster to start manufacturing in Canada. It is unlikely that any of them at that time suspected that the Canadian subsidiary was nothing more than a gigantic swindle. However, promotion material used in selling McKesson & Robbins stock had promised production by the crude-drug division, and Coster's associates thought the time had come to make good.

Coster assured them that he was working on a plan. He said that a Montreal bank had offered to put up $3,000,000 to build a plant if McKesson & Robbins could present a satisfactory proposal. Not long afterward a Canadian Press Service dispatch from Montreal reported plans for a million-dollar pharmaceutical factory in Canada. The story—planted by Coster—pointed out that Canadian tariff on a wide variety of drugs had been raised from 17.5 percent to 25.5 percent. Coster planted the story for several reasons. First, any plan for expansion implied economic health. Furthermore, it was not only good window-dressing for the Canadian subsidiary, but also it supported Coster's policies of keeping large inventories of crude drugs in Canadian warehouses and operations of the Canadian firm separate from the parent company.

McKesson & Robbins, Ltd., of Canada was now meticulously following all the proper practices and procedures of accountancy. Every month the accounting department at Fairfield received, through George Dietrich, a detailed statement from Manning & Co. reporting bills paid, moneys received from sales, balances credited to the crude-drug division in the private bank, and itemized inventories of drugs in Canadian warehouses.

When a "purchase" was planned, George Dietrich requested prices from the Canadian wholesalers. When a quotation had been selected, Robert Dietrich would prepare a formal purchase order in quadruplicate. George would sign these, keep the original for his files, "send" one to the nonexistent vendor, and send two to the bookkeeping and accounting departments. They were then entered on the books as valid transactions. An invoice always "came back" from the vendor to be filed as part of the record. Robert then made out a receipt ticket indicating that the merchandise was in the vendor's warehouse. The invoice was followed by a debit advice from the Manning bank showing that the seller had been paid.

Records of sales were kept with the same attention to detail. When a consignment of crude drugs was "sold," George Dietrich made out the factory order to which he attached two memoranda from W. W. Smith & Co. as sales agents for McKesson & Robbins, Ltd. These notes indicated that the sales had been made and the deliveries completed. All sales and purchases were made abroad, usually in some part of the British Empire. Copies of the sales orders were sent to the customers to inform them the goods had been shipped and to the billing department which then made out the invoice in seven copies. The original copy went to George Dietrich for mailing to the customer; he probably destroyed it immediately. One copy went to the bookkeeping department as a charge against the customer. The bill would go to W. W. Smith & Co. for collection. This was followed by an advice of credit from the trading agent stating that the customer had paid the bill and that the money had been deposited in the Manning bank. The Manning account in Fairfield would then reflect this credit.

Coster had a formal contract with W. W. Smith making that company sole agent for all crude-drug sales. The Smith firm guaranteed all accounts which in time numbered more than seven hundred, among them some of the most famous names in the pharmaceutical world. Smith received a fixed fee of $18,000 a year plus ¾ of 1 percent commission on sales.

During the slightly more than ten years of the Canadian operation, Coster sluiced some $120,000,000 in and out of the Smith accounts, most of it simultaneously flowing in and out of the McKesson & Robbins treasury.

Coster's colleagues were greatly impressed by his apparently expert knowledge of the international crude-drug market. They were awed by the erudition he displayed in casual references to Algerian rose-geranium oil, powdered Malayan dragon's blood, Peruvian balsam, or oil of East Indian sandalwood.

Coster was equally adept at name-dropping. "Mitsui is coming to New York next week," he once said to his brother George in the presence of some of his directors. "Remind me that I must see him and try to get a better price on Japanese camphor."

He had probably read of the impending visit of the multimillionaire Japanese industrialist. And who had not heard of the House of Mitsui, the Rothschilds of Japan, which controlled one-quarter of Japanese foreign trade, a vast share of the country's banking capital, to say nothing of mines, insurance companies, steel plants, mills, sugar refineries, a merchant fleet, and chemical works? It is highly unlikely that Coster had ever met any of the Mitsui clan, but on various tables of the villa on Mill Plain Road there were pictures of important-looking Japanese in kimono and haori who might well have been Mitsuis, as well as autographed photos of turbaned Hindus as regal as maharajas, mustachioed statesmen, high army officers in exotic uniforms, befezzed sultans who apparently controlled great forests that produced health-giving gums or oils or seeds.

Coster carried off his masquerade splendidly, but his homemade erudition did not filter down to his brothers George and Robert. Auditors, concerned exclusively with figures and documents, must have been so impressed by the exotic names on the inventories that they overlooked exaggeration of fact and errors of trade practice that almost anyone with a good background in crude drugs would have caught. What accountant would realize, for instance, that there were not enough Himalayan musk deer in the world to fill the orders placed by McKesson & Robbins, Ltd., for an essential oil derived from a particular gland in the males of these animals? Or that vanilla beans are shipped in tins and not in 200-pound bags like lima beans, as listed on the Canadian subsidiary's inventories? Or that the amount of procaine or iodoform supposedly stored in Canadian warehouses would supply the entire United States for years?

Robert Dietrich's lack of formal education was also reflected in some of his weird shipping instructions that were not discovered until years later. An observant auditor in the early '30's would have been suspicious of some of Robert's curious addresses that altered the world's geography. He might also have wondered about routing orders that moved merchandise from South America to Australia and China "by truck."

No one, apparently, wondered.

Coster must have had his tongue in his cheek when he wrote to his auditors, Price, Waterhouse, in 1933:

> Incidentally, our comptroller has called my attention to the fact that payments for auditing fees paid by us since organization to your good firm have reached the million mark. I am very glad of it and feel that among the major expenses incidental to mergers and consolidations only in auditing did our company really get its money's worth.

Coster must have got great personal satisfaction out of bamboozling his auditors. Anybody could fool rubes and nitwits, but cynical, sophisticated, coldly analytical types like bankers, brokers, attorneys, accountants and big-business executives had always been a special challenge to the boy from Mulberry Bend. The basis for this delight in making dupes of corporate characters is probably a well-thumbed book that was always handy in his desk—Merrill Goddard's *What Interests People and Why*. An underlined section must have strengthened Coster's faith in his own bold and unorthodox methods. It reads in part:

> It is the nationwide custom of banks and corporations to submit annual reports and financial statements, examined and approved by certified public accountants. Upon these sworn certificates, stockholders rely and investors base their judgment. . . .
>
> The truth which the public has never been told is that no practical system has ever been devised by which the complicated finances of a large institution can be thoroughly checked up so that every transaction is verified, except at prohibitive time and cost. . . .

Those lines explain how a reputable firm of auditors like the Price, Waterhouse company could be victimized into certifying the balance sheets first of the Girard company and then of McKesson & Robbins. Even in its earliest Coster transactions, Price, Waterhouse was retained only to make a check of accountancy for errors in calculation. The cost of verifying every W. W. Smith transaction with more than 700 worldwide accounts, checking the inventories in five Canadian warehouses, and tracing back every bookkeeping entry would have amounted to many times the million dollars

Coster paid the firm during the ten-year period to which his 1933 letter referred.

Price, Waterhouse could have learned much from its London branch about the techniques of hoodwinking a poor auditor. While Coster was masterminding his financial razzle-dazzle in America, a parallel performance was going on in Europe under the direction of Ivar Kreuger, the Swedish Match King. Until he shot himself through the heart in his Paris apartment on March 12, 1932, Kreuger was known as the "Golden Boy of International Finance," but the gold in the epithet soon proved to be base metal.

Less than a month after Kreuger's suicide, Price, Waterhouse, Ltd., was retained to unravel the incredibly tangled finances of the Swedish genius. The auditors quickly discovered that a substantial portion of Kreuger's putative great wealth was based on reports "greatly in excess of the items they purported to represent, entirely fictitious, or duplicative of assets belonging and appearing on the books of associated companies." There was also more than a soupçon of forgery and counterfeiting of securities involved.

The final report in which Price, Waterhouse, Ltd., listed the conditions that made possible Kreuger's gigantic swindle could easily have served to describe Coster's situation. The report read in part:

> The perpetration of frauds on so large a scale would have been impossible but for (1) the confidence which Kreuger [Coster] succeeded in inspiring, (2) the acceptance of his claim that complete secrecy in relation to vitally important transactions was essential to the success of the projects, (3) the autocratic powers which were conferred upon him, and (4) the loyalty or unquestioning obedience of officials.

Coster had been fascinated for years by the career of the

Swedish financier. He would frequently mention Kreuger's name, although he could hardly have known that there was any similarity in their methods. When he heard of Kreuger's death—he had not yet learned the man's success was largely based on fraud—he expressed a personal feeling of sadness to some of his associates. He showed little prescience when he said he was repelled by the idea that "such a man should find his end in the tragedy of suicide."

Meanwhile Coster continued to inspire confidence and loyalty while enjoying autocratic power to conduct the affairs of McKesson & Robbins, Ltd., Canada, in complete secrecy.

11 : The Lovely Face of Honesty

Wᴴɪʟᴇ the imaginary profits of the Canadian subsidiary continued to swell the balance sheet of McKesson & Robbins, Inc. (Maryland), Coster underwent a violent phase of honest enterprise. As years later his admirers liked to point out with rare hindsight, he was a true business genius whose only fault was that he found too much integrity galling.

The election of Franklin D. Roosevelt to the presidency in 1932 brought no joy to the heart of Coster, a confirmed Republican, but it showed him the way the winds of opinion were blowing. Roosevelt had campaigned as an out-and-out foe of Prohibition, and when he moved into the White House, the end of the bloody and lucrative reign of the bootlegger was in plain sight. The rich traffic in illicit alcohol that had launched Coster on his way to wealth and power and had helped McKesson & Robbins through the critical years would soon be coming to an end. When that happened, Coster would be ready.

Early in 1933 he created a planning board that worked out the organizational details of McKesson Spirits, Inc., in anticipation of the repeal of the Eighteenth Amendment. Preliminary work was done in Coster's suite at the Roosevelt Hotel in New York City under his personal direction. Later he rented office space in the Lincoln Building at 60 East 42d Street where a large staff worked feverishly to be ready to go the moment the sale of alcoholic beverages became legal.

As he had at each important step in his career, Coster again called on the urbane Julian Thompson for a special assignment. Thompson went abroad on a combination wine-tasting and contract-signing expedition. He toured the French vineyards with his shallow silver taster in one hand and a fountain pen in the other. He sipped his way from chateau to chateau in the Bordeaux region, looking for the exporter who would sell him the rights to some of the great clarets once Prohibition was declared dead. He rode through the rolling hills of Burgundy to attend the famous wine auction at Beaunes. He tramped miles through the underground cellars of Champagne, emerging triumphantly with the exclusive American rights to Pommery. Although his sophisticated Princetonian tastes led him tropismatically toward such great Burgundies as Corton, La Tache, and Montrachet, his business sense and his knowledge of the common denominator of American tastes moved him to sign a contract making McKesson & Robbins the sole United States agent for Chauvenet's Sparkling Burgundy.

When on December 5, 1933, Utah became the thirty-sixth state to ratify the Twenty-first Amendment (repealing the Eighteenth Amendment and nullifying the Volstead Act), McKesson & Robbins was in the liquor business legitimately. The firm not only had the valuable European agencies that

Thompson had brought home; it had, thanks to the merger plan, sixty-six ready-made distributing outlets stretching from coast to coast. Coster was in an admirable position to take immediate command of a large portion of the new and lucrative windfall market.

There was an added bonus. In addition to his own sales network, Coster had high-priority contacts with big-shot bootleggers who had also seen the handwriting on the wall and were busy learning to become legitimate businessmen dealing in the now-legal wines, beers, and spirits.

In the two years following Repeal, McKesson & Robbins' liquor-distributing subsidiary rang up gross sales of $22,000,-000. The curve rose steadily and at times sharply when more and more brands were added to the list. In 1936, McKesson & Robbins acquired the principal assets of Hunter Baltimore Rye Distillery. It was not long before Coster's foresight was bringing in $45,000,000 a year in liquor sales—all legal and aboveboard. Coster was smugly proud.

Had the boy from Mulberry Bend been familiar with the Elizabethan dramatists, he might have quoted from Thomas Dekker, author of *The Honest Whore*, who in the first years of the seventeenth century wrote: "Honest labor bears a lovely face."

Dr. F. Donald Coster hated Franklin D. Roosevelt and abhorred the New Deal with the combined violence and articulate fervor of a right-wing Republican, a corporation executive, and a Fairfield County millionaire. Whenever something displeased him in Washington, he wrote a special-delivery letter to the White House. When he went to the nation's capital on business, he spared no adjectives on New Deal underlings. But as well as a reactionary Republican, he was also a realist. While the Democrats were in power, it was not the Republicans who could help him when he needed political favors, which he frequently did.

Fortunately for McKesson & Robbins, the top men in the Department of Justice were Connecticut bigwigs: Attorney General Homer S. Cummings and his right-hand man, Assistant Attorney General Brien McMahon. And to avert the criticism that he by-passed the local sachems by going over their heads to the top brass, Coster made friends with one of the leading Democrats of the state, Archibald McNeil, a Democratic national committeeman.

McNeil, a former newspaper publisher and a member of one of the first families of Connecticut, was one of Franklin Roosevelt's original backers for the presidency. After Roosevelt was elected, he was McNeil's house guest every time he came into the state, and McNeil was a frequent White House guest during F.D.R.'s long tenure as President. As a national committeeman, he knew practically every figure of importance in Washington.

Coster put Archibald McNeil on the McKesson & Robbins payroll as public relations consultant at $5,000 a year.

However, the boy from Mulberry Bend had learned at an early age—when he was committed to the Elmira Reformatory, in fact—the value of having political contacts that were both sound and widespread. As a Republican he could not afford to ignore the hierarchy of his own political party, even if the Republicans were in eclipse in Connecticut as well as in Washington during the early Roosevelt years. So Coster cultivated Harry E. Mackenzie of Bethel, the Fairfield County Republican leader. Mackenzie, on a state level, was first lieutenant to J. Henry Roraback, the most powerful figure in Connecticut's political history. He was also a former labor commissioner, and, until Repeal, state Prohibition official for Connecticut.

Coster retained Harry Mackenzie as McKesson & Robbins lobbyist at $3,900 a year, plus $3,000 annually for expenses.

When the president of McKesson & Robbins spoke his mind on matters of patronage or legislation, both state and national, he expected to be heard. And he did not hesitate to make his wishes known on any question pertaining to the drug or liquor business. Although he was a reticent host who entertained rarely, his limited hospitality was a happy asset politically. His very private and select dinner parties, with the finest food and wines followed by rare old brandy and the most fragrant cigars, were social and epicurean adventures. An invitation to one was a status symbol that Coster never cheapened. Only those who could deliver favors were welcome. When he entertained a politician lavishly, he expected lavish returns and he was not shy about demanding his *quid pro quo*. His attitude in this connection can be illustrated with utmost clarity by a letter he once wrote to a political friend:

Dear——

I am beginning to lose faith in the ability of the Democratic Party to deliver. It seems their idea of delivery is . . . attractive dinners attended by attractive personalities . . . more talking than delivery, which may be perfectly fine and interesting to some people, but it doesn't interest me.

Recently a request was made to favor a certain doctor in Bridgeport through an appointment by the Governor's office, and nothing has been done; but more annoying, the Governor vetoed the liquor bill compelling retailers to pay their bills within fifteen days. Both matters, I was very interested in, so . . . we had better adopt the policy of performance first and payment after, rather than vice versa, in the future.

F. DONALD COSTER

Another letter from about the same period confirmed succinctly Coster's point of view on matters political. One phrase summed up his pragmatic philosophy:

> We hope to avoid in the future difficulties with inexperienced government officials who fail to see the practical side of our problems.

This letter was accompanied by a check for $5,000. The voucher in the McKesson & Robbins accounting department supporting this particular check listed the item as "Original payment as tax consultant, Federal, State." If Coster was true to his philosophy of "payment first," we may assume that the "practical side of our problems" had been satisfactorily delivered before the check was drawn.

Coster's political connections were particularly useful in meeting complications arising from the sprawling monster that his merger project had become. In the early 1930's, the selling arm of McKesson & Robbins, Inc. (Maryland) comprised sixty-six large regional distributors and employed 700 drug salesmen and served 5,500 retail drugstores from coast to coast. It had become truly the colossus of the pharmaceutical industry.

The owners of the regional wholesale firms who had taken McKesson & Robbins stock in return for their interests in their own companies had become salaried vice presidents of the Maryland holding company. The imposing list contained such distinguished names in the industry as J. B. Bedsole, Frank E. Bogart, Warren N. Churchill, Charles F. Cutler, Sewall Gurler, George V. Doerr, George B. Evans, Henry D. Faxon, W. F. Geary, William W. Gibson, B. B. Gilmer, C. F. Michaels, James W. Morrisson, William J. Murray, Jr., E. B.

Patten, L. D. Sale, Ludwig Schiff, and A. H. Van Gorder. As the corporate structure grew, the board of directors grew to a membership of thirty, including nine bankers. The firm also accumulated an unwieldy list of 200 officers, including some eighty vice presidents.

Most of the vice presidents had come into the merger on the general understanding that they would continue to have a free hand in running their family businesses in their own territories. They were shocked and not a little mutinous when they discovered that Coster's corporate design called for a highly centralized control system, and that the controls were to be tightly held in his own autocratic hand. Since he owned 10 percent of the outstanding common stock, however, there was nothing much to prevent his acting as arbitrary captain of this crew of former independents.

The problem of his vice presidents did not worry Coster unduly. He considered them stodgy and unimaginative and incapable of coming up with any ideas even faintly approaching his own. He was, however, somewhat bothered by his corporate image in the view of the retail drug trade. McKesson & Robbins had long been identified in the trade as a relentless foe of the drugstore chains and a fast friend of the independent retailer. On the other hand, Coster's long-range plans involved a direct assault on the consumer market, with McKesson & Robbins products going directly from the Fairfield factory to company-owned retailers. His new colleagues, the wholesaling vice presidents, trained in the field, were rebellious at the thought of wholesalers and jobbers going into the retail business. They were also dubious about his plans for simplifying the nearly 50,000 items on the list of manufactured pharmaceutical products being handled by the merged wholesalers.

Neither objection proved a serious obstacle. Coster continued to pose as an enemy of the drugstore chains while laying plans to organize his own chain of retailers. Anti-chain McKesson & Robbins would not appear in the scheme at all. The stores would be acquired by the Consolidated Investment Corporation, a dummy company that would provide Coster with a façade while McKesson & Robbins preserved its own corporate image by subsidizing a nation-wide campaign in support of anti-chain-store legislation.

Independent retailers were delighted by the full-page advertisements sponsored by McKesson & Robbins that appeared in all the trade journals. They were even more delighted when Coster retained Congressman Wright Patman, Texas Democrat and co-author of the Robinson-Patman anti-chain-store act, for a coast-to-coast lecture tour. Double-truck spreads appeared in trade publications, carrying Congressman Patman's picture and explaining that the educational lecture tour was to "consolidate the sentiment of retailers, manufacturers and businessmen generally behind the Robinson-Patman Act for the elimination of discrimination between customers, and the establishment of fair play in business." The advertisement complimented Patman and unabashedly took credit for his tour. The congressman, in turn, was high in his praise of McKesson & Robbins as a courageous foe of chain-store operations. Coster's paternalistic portrait thus continued undimmed among the independents all the while he was preparing to gobble them up.

Coster's dream was complete domination of all phases of the drug business. He kept prodding his wholesale outlets to get more McKesson & Robbins products into the field, even if it meant extending risky credit to retailers. His urging paid off in greatly expanded sales of company products, although the Depression years exacted their toll. The cost of easy consumer credit in 1933: McKesson & Robbins wrote off $3,000,000 in bad debts.

When the wholesaling vice presidents' opposition to Coster's proposed plan to trim and streamline the nearly 50,000 varieties of drugs, remedies, and cosmetics handled by the giant holding company reached serious proportions, the president took countermeasures. He was determined to eliminate duplications, to weed out slow-selling items, to simplify bookkeeping by simplifying the list, and to promote his Fairfield products over similar remedies previously favored by the regional family firms. Coster therefore proposed a survey by outside experts. He himself named the experts: Waddill Catchings, a former director and an alumnus of Goldman, Sachs; Maynard Bird of Bond & Goodwin; and Grant Keehn, also an ex-Goldman, Sachs man. From the record, it seems obvious that Coster expected to keep a tight control over this trio. Their report confirmed his confidence. They reported that McKesson & Robbins' troubles could be blamed on the wholesale houses with their stagnant inventories, high overhead, duplication of effort, and extravagant credits (which Coster himself had encouraged).

The next step was the appointment of a committee to devise a constructive program which would eliminate the curable ills the previous group had pointed out. Catchings was named to head the group, which included Coster himself as well as seven of the wholesalers who had been opposing his streamlining plans as aimed directly at their private fiefs. As Catchings began to hear their side of the story, he apparently sensed a revolt brewing against the Liege Lord of Fairfield. He was intrigued but his curiosity did him little good.

Coster had intended that Catchings confine his recommendations to the operations of the holding company—McKesson & Robbins, Inc. (Maryland). When Catchings began to look into the operations of McKesson & Robbins of Connecticut, Coster's personal domain, the friendly relationship between Catchings and the president deteriorated rapidly. His quest for information and statistics related to the manufacturing, purchasing, and selling activities of the Fairfield plant got little cooperation from the front office.

There is nothing to indicate that Catchings' curiosity was inspired by anything but the desire to do a thorough job, but Coster was evidently not only resentful of his digging into the Fairfield operation but also suspicious of his possible further probing into the Canadian subsidiary. After a few months of frustrating effort to get cooperation from top management, and getting only stony scorn from the man who had appointed him, Catchings became completely disenchanted with Coster. Convinced that the genius was a poor executive, he sent a report to individual members of the board of directors, declaring that he found the business in "the most chaotic condition" he had ever seen. The report contained equally blunt phrases such as "certain weaknesses . . . erratic and ill-considered action . . . devious ways. . . ." His devastating summary strongly urged the ousting of the president, declaring flatly: "There is no further place in the McKesson & Robbins organization for F. D. Coster."

The Catchings report was of course bound to reach Coster, although it was not addressed to him. When it did, he erupted fire and brimstone. He caught the first train for Manhattan and established his command post at the Roosevelt Hotel, a few angry steps from the holding company's executive offices at 155 East 44th Street. He immediately polled the board.

Catchings, he was not surprised to find, had not only polled the board before him but had been also campaigning vigorously for his ouster. The boy from Mulberry Bend took appropriate countersteps. He did not have to convince the Connecticut bankers that he was a financial wizard; they had proof of his wizardry in dollars and cents. The New York financiers, impressed both by Julian Thompson's enthusiasm for Coster and by Coster's apparent knowledge of the international crude-drug market, of which they knew nothing except what was reflected on the balance sheet, were also easily convinced that Catchings was a self-seeking trouble-maker fomenting revolt in the hope of moving in on a good thing. Coster next turned his charm on the dissidents, and Catchings was through. The president charmed his birds out of the trees and caged them.

A big majority of the board still convinced that their president was a genius reelected him enthusiastically. Catchings pocketed his fee of $35,000 for seven months of fruitless effort and departed. He had cried "wolf" and the sheep had laughed him off the field.

12 : The Frightened Yachtsman

I<small>N</small> 1934, Coster achieved the *ne plus ultra* of status symbols: a seagoing yacht. He purchased the craft for $40,-000 from John Hayes Hammond, American yachtsman and inventor, a colleague of the Nobel-prize-winning pioneer of wireless telegraphy, Guglielmo Marconi. Hammond had used the yacht as a floating laboratory for his experiments with radio-controlled planes, surface ships, and submarines, often with Marconi aboard. While it was not an old vessel (it had been built in the Kiel shipyards of the famous Krupp Steel Works), it had explored the Amazon and sailed around the world several times. Coster immediately rechristened the yacht *Carolita* in honor of his wife.

The *Carolita* was a twin-screw oil burner. She measured slightly more than 123 feet overall, with a beam of 23 feet, a draft of 12½ feet, and a gross tonnage of 284. Coster spent more than twice the purchase price in converting her from a pelagic experimental station to a luxury craft. He rebuilt and redecorated her completely below decks, putting in teakwood fittings, an elaborate lounge and dining saloon, elegant staterooms that would sleep twelve guests, modern baths that ran hot and cold, fresh and salt, water, and two-way radio communication. He reconditioned the engines, refitted the galley, and refurbished the bar and dining saloon with china, silver, and glassware designed to dazzle the beholder—which it did. The yacht was finally repainted a conservative jet black.

Captain William Baker commanded a crew of eleven while cruising in Long Island Sound, fourteen when he took the *Carolita* into blue water. Coster bought himself a yachting cap and hoisted the burgees of the New York Yacht Club and the Black Rock Yacht Club of Bridgeport, two of the most exclusive in the East.

The burgees were symbols, like membership in the swank clubs to which Coster belonged: the New York Bankers Club, the Lotos Club, the University Club, the Brooklawn Country Club. He rarely was seen in any clubhouse, but he paid his dues and he wanted the privilege of taking a Senator or an important banker to lunch at one of them if he felt like it. And he could really see how far he had come from Mulberry Bend when he cruised down Long Island Sound and gave orders to drop anchor among the yachts of the Morgans, the Vanderbilts, and the George Bakers.

The *Carolita,* however, was more than a symbol; she was a refuge, an island to which Coster could retreat safe in the knowledge that the ghosts of his past could not follow him there. When he invited two or three couples, colleagues perhaps, or financiers, or useful politicians, he knew he could cruise the Sound, or the New England coast as far as Maine, or South with the robins in winter if the Gulf Stream beckoned, without fear of being confronted by the specters of

Mulberry Bend, Elmira, or the Tombs. For all his arrogance, his cold-blooded aloofness, and his pseudo-Prussian authoritarianism, Dr. F. Donald Coster was a man afraid, desperately afraid.

Some of his associates—he had no friends—who were invited for dinner or a short cruise aboard the *Carolita,* have remarked on the sea change that used to come over Coster the moment he had given the order to cast off and could feel the deck throbbing to the pulse of the engines. The thin-lipped iciness seemed to melt. He would take a drink without a preliminary discourse on the subject of ulcers. He even laughed. And while he would order crew members to haul in the fish his guests had hooked, he would unbend, on occasion, to the extent of going into the galley to taste the spaghetti sauce his cook was whipping up. The fact that he would tolerate Italian food publicly was an indication of how secure he felt aboard his yacht. Nobody could walk out of his past, board the *Carolita,* and tap him on the shoulder without warning.

The streets of New York City were full of terror for him. When business forced him to travel to the city, he would always ride in the first car of the train, thus shortening his walk through the underground passages of Grand Central Station to the adjacent Hotel Roosevelt, where he always stayed. He ordered his meals sent to his suite to avoid appearing in a public dining room. On the rare occasions when he consented to lunch with his fellow executives, the others noted that on the way to and from the restaurant, Coster always walked a short distance apart from the group. Some of the men at first interpreted his actions as another sign of his snobbish aloofness, but later, as one of them recalled it, "we guessed that the great man was just absorbed in thought."

None of them could have imagined how alone and frightened the great man felt on the city streets.

For all his caution, Coster could not entirely avoid his great enemy Philip Musica. One day he was hurrying through Grand Central Station to catch his train for Fairfield when he heard someone call out: "Hello there, Phil."

Francis X. Hobs, III, who had known Coster as Philip Musica right after his release from the Tombs in 1916, was surprised to see Coster hurry even faster, as though he had heard nothing. Hobs stepped up his own pace and put his hand on Coster's arm.

"Hello, Phil. How are you?"

Coster turned in apparent surprise. "Oh, hello, Hobs," he said coolly. Then, for no evident reason, he added, "I'm working for Henry Ford out in Detroit now," and dashed off for his train.

Hobs later remembered wondering why Coster had volunteered this odd bit of information in return for a casual greeting, but attached no special significance to it at the time.

Closely coupled with Coster's fear of being recognized as Musica was the knowledge that Musica was still technically a fugitive from justice. The charge of subornation of perjury, dating back to Musica's near-successful efforts in 1921 to send Joseph Cohen to the electric chair for murder, was still hanging over him. Coster's maneuvers to get that indictment quashed provided a deep insight into the perverse psychology of the born adventurer. While his every action showed that he was almost constantly afraid, there was little doubt that he actually thrived on fear. While he scurried through the underground passages of Grand Central Station like a hunted animal to avoid being recognized, he would also respond to the adventurer's urge to go out of his way in courting danger.

The man who had originally demanded that Philip Musica be indicted for subornation of perjury was Attorney Jonah H. Goldstein, brilliant New York trial lawyer, who had led the fight to save Joseph Cohen from the electric chair. Who then, Coster must have argued with himself, would be a more appropriate man to quash the indictment than Jonah Goldstein himself?

One day in 1929 Coster walked into Goldstein's law offices, identified himself as Philip Musica, a poor ice peddler, and asked for legal representation. His accent and his worn work clothes did not impress the underlings with his importance. The case was certainly not important enough to bother the senior partner with, so it was handed to Attorney Albert de Roose, one of the younger members of the firm, to whom the name Musica meant nothing. After two appearances in the Court of General Sessions, Attorney de Roose persuaded Judge William Allen to dismiss the indictment.

During this same period the files on Philip Musica's early hocus-pocus with Italian cheese and human hair also disappeared from both the district attorney's office and the records of the clerk of the Court of General Sessions. The exact technique by which Coster accomplished this feat of legerdemain has never been revealed. However, in those happy-go-lucky days of the Jimmy Walker administration, the most unlikely characters—even newspaper reporters—used to rove at will through the files of both the police department and the halls of justice.

Although after 1929 Coster was no longer a fugitive from justice, he was still very much a fugitive from his past. Besides his family and Carol Hubbard, however, there was one figure from his past for whom he stood still—Benjamin Simon.

Simon had been associated with Coster during his Spe-cial-Investigator-Johnson masquerade and the poultry-war murders. He had also been president of the Adelphi Phar-maceutical firm when Coster, as Costa, had been involved with the Brandinos in providing bootleggers with alcohol. After Simon had helped his friend dispose of the Brandinos, he used the knowledge acquired during his investigation of the Baff murder to muscle in on the poultry trade. He did so well among the chicken dealers that in a few years he became the czar of the fowl markets. His czardom came to a sudden end when he was arrested and convicted of violating the Sher-man Antitrust Act. When he completed his three-month prison term, he called on his old friend Coster, who had also come a long way since their early association.

There is no evidence that Simon tried to blackmail Coster, although he certainly made a good thing out of renewing old ties. Some of Coster's petty underworld cronies were begin-ning to come out of the woodwork during the last years of Prohibition, among them the Brandinos. And since Simon had once shown his ability to handle the tough, unscrupulous brother and sister, Coster welcomed his reappearance and immediately put him to work as buffer, bodyguard, and gen-eral factotum for miscellaneous skulduggery.

Simon went on the McKesson & Robbins payroll at $6,000 a year, and drew paychecks for similar amounts under each of two pseudonyms. Simon had a fine assortment of aliases that he drew on to fit the assignments Coster gave him. He was known as Harold Redmond, George Goulet, L. Hartman, and, on at least one occasion, Philip M. Musica. He was also an officer in several companies doing business with McKesson & Robbins, most of them outlets for diverting alcohol into illegal channels during the last years of Prohibition. The firms bore such names as Simon Brothers, Rameses, Inc., Woodtone Company, and the Liberty Drug & Chemical Company.

Simon got such top-secret jobs as the forgery of counterfeit documents. When Coster was preparing to alter his family tree, he insisted that all basic papers should support his new identity and those of his family. Ben Simon got the assignment to prepare false birth certificates for Coster and the two Dietrichs. Armed with forged affidavits signed by an "Adele Vinard, midwife," of 1840 Grand Concourse, the Bronx (Simon's own address), Simon took off for Washington, D. C., the city Coster had chosen to be his birthplace. At exactly 11:50 A.M. on the morning of August 7, 1935, Simon registered the affidavits with the Bureau of Vital Statistics of the District of Columbia. The affiant swore that she had brought Frank Donald Coster into the world in Washington, D.C., on May 12, 1884; George Edmund Dietrich on February 22, 1894, and Robert Dietrich on March 18, 1900.

Coster's parents were registered as Anthony and Marie Girard Coster. (A few years later when he submitted his biographical sketch to *Who's Who in America* "Coster" changed his father's name from Anthony to Frank Donald.) Coster *père*'s occupation was given as chemist, and his birthplace recorded as 125 A Street, N.E., Washington, D.C., which happened to be the site of the then-new Supreme Court Building. The parents of the brothers Dietrich were identified as George Dietrich, a clerk, born in New York City, and Alice B. Miller Dietrich of Boston. Ben Simon's imagination was worthy of Coster's confidence.

Simon was a master at dealing with the scrubby blackmailers who were drawn to the blaze of Coster's new name and opulence like ants to a picnic. Most of those who knew Coster as Musica were easy to get rid of. Misfits and failures even in their chosen fields of crime, they were timorous and furtive, handicapped by fears of reprisal, legal or lethal. Simon paid them off with paltry sums and a warning.

The Brandinos were bolder and more persistent. They had never forgiven Coster for having wrecked the Adelphi Pharmaceutical firm, and they sensed that he was terrified of being unmasked. At first they made sporadic appearances at Fairfield, haunting the McKesson & Robbins gates so that he could not fail to see them, standing silently like ghosts from the past, as he entered or left his offices. Then they sent pleas for small loans to meet emergencies: they faced eviction because their rent was overdue, there was no coal in the dead of winter, or they had big medical expenses. They thought the device of requesting loans would protect them from charges of blackmail, but they reckoned without Simon, for they were subsequently (after the resurrection of Philip Musica) indicted and convicted.

Simon assumed Philip Musica's discarded identity when a New Orleans lawyer, trying to collect a debt dating back to the flight and capture following the collapse of the United States Hair Company, was on the point of pinning the claim on Coster. Ben Simon led the bloodhounds off the scent with a trail of greenbacks.

One man who learned Coster's true identity but made no attempt to capitalize on it was George H. Cohen, a former Assistant United States Attorney practicing law in Hartford, Connecticut. Cohen was asked by Brooklyn Attorney Charles Berlin to bring suit against Coster to collect a $20,000 debt. Berlin's client, one Alfred Vitale of Brooklyn, claimed that Philip Musica had borrowed the money while connected with the Adelphi Pharmaceutical Manufacturing Company, had disappeared without paying back the loan, and had now re-appeared as F. Donald Coster. While Cohen was preparing the papers for the action, Coster apparently got wind of the matter and rushed Simon to Brooklyn. Before Cohen could file suit he was informed by his Brooklyn correspondent that Vitale had settled the case for $7,500. The Hartford lawyer later explained that he had kept Coster's secret for two reasons: first, he considered the matter of his identity a confidential matter between attorneys, and, second, he felt that Coster's amazing rehabilitation had earned him the right to privacy.

Another who had followed Philip Musica's rise to fame and fortune and who had done nothing to betray his masquerade as Coster was Edward Hubbard, the man Philip had driven to the verge of madness because he coveted his wife. If any man had reason to unmask Coster, if only for revenge if not for profit, it was Hubbard. Carol Jenkins Hubbard Coster's first husband, however, was not bitter. He had made a new life for himself, such as it was, and whatever he thought of Coster, he wished Carol happiness.

However, Hubbard had a new wife. After Carol had divorced him, he had married a friend of hers, Irene Wolf, the girl who had sung in the Brooklyn choir with Carol. They had accumulated a family of five children and an impressive pile of debts when the second Mrs. Hubbard learned that the first Mrs. Hubbard was married to a millionaire corporation executive. She had come across a curious document whereby Hubbard had somehow transferred surrender value of an insurance policy to the original beneficiary, first wife Carol. Why should this asset belong to the mink-draped wife of a Croesus while the Hubbards were behind in the mortgage payments on their home in Jamaica, Long Island, and the children were rapidly growing into the expensive age groups? Hubbard reluctantly wrote to Coster in Fairfield. Although Hubbard recognized the justice of his second wife's argument, all fight had gone out of him since he had lost his business and Carol.

Coster had an underling—probably Simon—telephone the Hubbards, asking them to call a New York City number. They did.

"Dr. Coster would be glad to see you," said a voice. "When could you come to Fairfield?"

With unexpected spunk, Hubbard said that it would be inconvenient for them to go to Fairfield, but that if Dr. Coster were really interested, Mr. and Mrs. Hubbard would be happy to see him in their Jamaica home. The Costers accepted the invitation.

There was an air of suspense surrounding the modest Jamaica home of the Hubbards as the chauffeur-driven Lincoln drew up to the curb. There was a flutter of curtains at the second-floor windows as the five children, consigned to limbo for the fateful interview, tried to observe the cause of their exclusion from family life. There was a tense moment as the prosperous-looking couple from Connecticut walked from the expensive car to the lower middle-class front porch. The first Mrs. Hubbard lagged a few steps behind her husband, who was in complete command of the situation.

"Ed," said Coster, holding out his hand, "it's good to see you again. There's no reason we four can't be friends. Let's live and let live. Shall we let bygones be bygones?"

The Hubbards were obviously not going to break off diplomatic relations on the front porch. In the Grand Rapids atmosphere of the living room, Coster laughed off the matter of the insurance policy as a misunderstanding. Of course, it should have been transferred to the present Mrs. Hubbard.

"Irene—if you will let me call you that," said Coster in his most charming manner, "I want you to accept my apologies—and this check."

The check took care of the money involved—plus interest accrued. There were smiles. The tension was suddenly lifted.

"Ed," said Coster, "you're not looking well. Your old hay fever must be still with you. How can a man take care of his family when he's not in good health? Ed, the climate around here is no good for you." Coster shook his head sympathetically. The climate was not good for Coster either, so long as Ed Hubbard lived so close to Fairfield County, Ed Hubbard who knew his history from the Great Hair Hoax onward. "You'll have to let me help fix you up, Ed. We'll be in touch with you soon."

The parting was friendly. As the sleek Lincoln pulled away, the hard-pressed Hubbards smiled for the first time in months.

A week or so later Coster's emissary called at the Hubbard home in Jamaica. This time it was not Simon. Coster chose an envoy known to—and, he thought, trusted by—Hubbard: Carol's brother, Leonard Jenkins. Hubbard knew that his ex-brother-in-law had long suffered from a bad sinus ailment, so it made sense when Jenkins suggested that they both seek a more salubrious climate, where they could go into business together.

"Marvelous idea," agreed the hay-fever victim, "but what do we use for money?"

"Don't worry about money," Jenkins assured him. "Worry about your allergy and I'll worry about my sinuses."

Neither man mentioned the source of the money, and Hubbard, although he did not ask, suspected that Coster might be having a twinge of conscience. Even then he could not believe that a man could be completely without conscience, that Coster was cold-bloodedly acting only in his own self-interest. Hubbard did not know that Jenkins had developed into a complete ineffectual parasite.

Jenkins was on the McKesson & Robbins payroll at $35 a week as a messenger and general roustabout. And, since he was also Coster's brother-in-law, there were brokerage accounts in his name in Wall Street, and he drove a fine, high-powered car. Hubbard accepted the proposition that he accompany Jenkins on an expedition in search of a healthier climate that would provide business opportunities for both of them. After all, anything was better than looking into the eyes of growing children who were getting barely enough to eat.

The two men were gone ten weeks on their scouting trip. Jenkins picked Reading, Pennsylvania, as a promising city with a climate favorable to hay-fever and sinus sufferers. It also offered an opportunity to buy into a going electrical and radio supply business. Inasmuch as Jenkins was furnishing the capital, Hubbard could hardly object. He moved his family to Reading.

Years later, Hubbard found it difficult to remember exactly what happened next. Everything was confusing. He recalled only that he seemed to have lost his old business acumen and that Leonard Jenkins (with a characteristic ineptitude then unknown to Hubbard) did everything wrong. The end was inevitable.

When the venture finally collapsed, Jenkins disappeared, and Hubbard found himself stranded in a small town called Breinigsville, Pennsylvania, ten miles outside of Allentown, in the heart of the Pennsylvania Dutch country. He and his large and growing family—Irene had by now presented him with his sixth and seventh children—lived rent-free in a house that belonged to Carol Coster, his first wife.

Things were tough all over in those Depression years and Breinigsville, Pennsylvania, was no exception. For a while, Hubbard managed to provide for Irene and the children at subsistence level by working as a handyman in nearby towns. When the New Deal invented the Work Progress Administration to make jobs for the jobless, Edward Hubbard, the once-prosperous Wall Street broker, took a W.P.A. assignment.

The boy from Mulberry Bend had laid another ghost from the past.

13 : The Dilettante Gunrunner

THE MOST astounding hush-hush project on which Ben Simon did the legwork for Coster was a cloak-and-dagger venture in international intrigue involving enough small arms to equip a modern force of more than a hundred divisions.

If Simon could find a likely customer, Coster proposed to sell some 2,000,000 rifles to "friendly, nonbelligerent consignees, whose ambassadors will attest cognizance of the order being delivered to such consignees." At least so read the contract drawn up at Coster's request by Attorney Frederic Wingersky, a highly regarded Boston lawyer who served as vice president in charge of McKesson & Robbins' legal department. The rifles—2,300,000 Lee-Enfields—were the property of the United States government, surplus from World War I, stored in various warehouses. They had been manufactured originally for shipment to Great Britain in 1917, but when the United States entered the war in April of that year, they were withheld for use by American troops. Very few of the Lee-Enfields ever saw action, however, as U.S. arsenals were turning out the standard Springfield rifles as fast as the American Expeditionary Force could be organized and trained. When the United States Senate rejected Wilson, the Versailles Treaty, and internationalism, the country withdrew into isolation and the regular army shrank to few more than 100,000 men. Our arsenals bulged with nearly two dozen rifles for every soldier.

As the stated value of the rifles was $29,000,000, the interest and avarice that stirred in the hearts of those to whom Coster mentioned this project can well be imagined. Wingersky was instructed to turn the contract over to Ben Simon, who thereupon was promoted from "chief of the secret service" to "foreign minister." The names of the contracting parties were left blank on the document, except that the "Standard Oil Company of England" was mentioned as a principal in the deal. There was no such company in existence at that time—except in Coster's fantastic imagination.

The lengthy contract ran to more than 1200 words and spelled out in detail the intricate financial agreement. It also included an explicit description of the guns that read in part as follows:

> Absolutely new Lee-Enfield rifles; 1917 and 1919 manufacture; packed in original cases, twenty to a case; complete with bayonet, sling, scabbard, cleaning rod and depression follower; glycerine or cosmoline packed; a specific number of one hundred thousand cartridges for same. . . .

The contract also specified that all merchandise be delivered free of charge to arsenals or warehouses within 1,500 miles of New York, or to American ports on the Eastern seaboard, for delivery to British ports designated by the purchaser.

"Dr. F. Donald Coster" (*né* Philip Musica), president of McKesson & Robbins and Fairfield squire, poses here (*left*), on the sun porch of his Fairfield, Connecticut, Italianate villa (*below*), with one of Carol Coster's prize-winning chows. Musica had come a long way from the crowded flat on Mulberry Bend, New York City, in which he was born.

Carol Jenkins Hubbard Coster *(left)* loved pretty clothes. Here she was photographed resplendent in the finery "Daddy Coster" lavishly supplied.

When Musica filled out his application for a marriage license *(right)*, he was his usual self, ready and willing to falsify information. From his own name to the date of Carol Hubbard's divorce, there are few true facts.

STATE OF NEW YORK

Affidavit for License to Marry

Musica's 125-foot *Carolita (above)*, flying the burgees of the New York and Black Rock yacht clubs, steams out of port. In the ship's dining room *(top)* Musica played host to top financiers and politicians. In his stateroom *(center)* Musica felt secure from the always-present threat of being unmasked. Commanding the *Carolita*'s eleven-man crew *(bottom)* was a particular delight to the "boy from Mulberry Bend."

PLACE OF BIRTH
District of Columbia

HEALTH DEPARTMENT, DISTRICT OF COLUMBIA
Certificate of Birth

Registration No.

381,879-D

Dist. No.

125 - A St. N.E.
(Give street, number, and section)

Use this form ONLY in case of a live birth (1):
in other cases use the form provided for the reporting
of STILLBIRTHS. No report need be made of a
stillbirth when the fetus has apparently not passed
the fifth month of gestation.
If a stillbirth occurs in the practice of a midwife
she must report it IMMEDIATELY to the Coroner.
This may be done through the nearest police station.

HEALTH DEPARTMENT
(Reserved for use of Health Department)

Time of Receipt

1935 AUG 7 AM 11 50

(Name of institution, if any)

Full name of child *Frank Donald Coster*
(If not named when this report is made, parents should make a supplemental report. See instructions on back.)

| Sex of child *male* | Twin, triplet, or other? No. in order of birth .... (To be answered only in the event of plural births) | Legitimate Yes. No. Unknown. | Date of birth *May 12th*, 19*1884* (Month) (Day) (Year) |

FATHER

Full name *Anthony Coster*
Residence *125 - A St. N.E.*
Color *White* Age last birthday *39* years
Birthplace *Baltimore Md.*
Occupation *Chemist*

MOTHER

Full maiden name *Marie Girard*
Residence *125 - A St. N.E.*
Color *White* Age last birthday *25* years
Birthplace *Baltimore, Md.*
Occupation *housewife*

No. of children born to this mother, including present birth *One*
No. of children of this mother now living *One*

CERTIFICATE OF ATTENDING PHYSICIAN OR MIDWIFE

I HEREBY CERTIFY that I attended at the birth of this child, that it occurred on the date above stated, at *5 a.* m.,
that the child was born alive (1), and that the above information, in so far as not based upon my personal observation, was
furnished by *Anthony Coster*, whose relationship to this child is that of *father*
and whose address is *125 - A St. N.E.*

Signature of *Adele Vinard* (Physician or Midwife)

Dated *Aug 6th 1935* Address *1840 Grand Concourse, N.Y. city N.Y.*

Instructions—(1) A child is born alive if it breathes or shows any other evidence of life after the child is altogether outside of the mother's body.
(2) In case of multiple births a SEPARATE RETURN must be made for each, and the number of each in order of birth stated.
(3) A child is legitimate if either conceived or born in wedlock. Draw a line through the words not needed. For instructions as
to reporting illegitimate births, see Act printed on back of this blank.

WRITE PLAINLY WITH UNFADING INK. THIS IS A PERMANENT RECORD

RESERVED FOR OFFICIAL USE

Another sample of Musica's improvising is the birth certificate *(above)* he had filed in Washington in 1935. With a few strokes of a pen the Italian-born barber Antonio Musica became the Baltimore-born chemist Anthony Girard!

Julian Thompson *(right)*, Princetonian, Wall Street investment banker, and McKesson & Robbins' treasurer, was one of the first to recognize Musica's genius. His suspicions led him to destroy the mythical titan he had helped create.

There was nothing fictitious about the plant of McKesson & Robbins in Fairfield, Connecticut. Here Musica centralized McKesson & Robbins' manufacturing facilities and administrative offices. The chart compares Musica's fantasy structure with the corporation that actually existed.

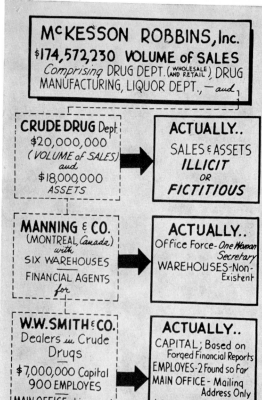

McKESSON ROBBINS, Inc.
$174,572,230 VOLUME of SALES
Comprising DRUG DEPT. (WHOLESALE AND RETAIL) DRUG MANUFACTURING, LIQUOR DEPT., — and

CRUDE DRUG Dept.
$20,000,000
(VOLUME of SALES)
and
$18,000,000
ASSETS

ACTUALLY..
SALES & ASSETS
ILLICIT
OR
FICTITIOUS

MANNING & CO.
(MONTREAL, Canada)
with
SIX WAREHOUSES
FINANCIAL AGENTS for

ACTUALLY..
Office Force- One Woman Secretary
WAREHOUSES- Non-Existent

W.W. SMITH & CO.
Dealers in Crude Drugs
$7,000,000 Capital
900 EMPLOYES
MAIN OFFICE, Liverpool
AGENTS- Throughout the world

ACTUALLY..
CAPITAL; Based on Forged Financial Reports
EMPLOYES- 2 Found so far
MAIN OFFICE- Mailing Address Only
AGENTS- One in Montreal and one in Brooklyn

After the suicide of their brother Philip, the three Musica brothers —(*left to right*) Robert, Arthur, and George—pleaded guilty in the New York Federal Court to charges of violating the Securities Act of 1934.

Mary Brandino (*right*) was photographed as she was indicted by a Brooklyn, New York, grand jury for blackmailing her former bootlegging partner, Philip Musica.

New York District Attorney Thomas E. Dewey and Assistant District Attorney Sewall T. Tying *(above)* examine the fraudulent McKesson & Robbins papers that Musica so ingeniously prepared. In 1909, Musica *(see police photo below)* was sentenced to Elmira Reformatory for bribing customs inspectors.

Louise Musica (Mrs. Robert Guex), the oldest of the Musica girls, was questioned during the 1938 investigation of Musica, though she was the only member of the family who had broken away from Philip's aegis.

The famous "As God is my judge" suicide note *(below)* was written by Philip Musica after the fraudulent crude-drug division was exposed. Writing his own epitaph, "Coster" claimed he was "a victim of Wall Street plunder and blackmail."

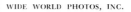

Coster brought some of his influential political friends into the picture. There was sufficient loot in the filibuster for everyone. The role of the politicos was simple but essential. All they had to do was to have the rifles condemned. The security measures protecting the transaction were so perfect that no hint of it reached the public until years later. Government officials then denied that the rifles had been made available to anyone, but Thomas A. Bruni of New York City, industrial engineer and arms broker, testified under oath that considerable progress had been made on a sale of 200,000 guns to Chiang Kai-shek.

Chiang rejected the deal at the last moment, it was said, on the grounds that the rifles were obsolete and of different caliber from those then used by his troops. The difference in caliber, he explained, would complicate Chiang's problem of ammunition supply. Another version of the collapse of the sale to China blamed Chiang's withdrawal on his failure to get a United States subsidy for the arms purchase. American credit was apparently the carrot dangled by Coster's agents before the Chinese. Since there was no declared war between China and Japan at the time, despite the fighting in North China and the Yangtze Valley, China was considered a non-belligerent nation under the Neutrality Act, and the sale of Lee-Enfields would have been legal. However, Coster's Washington friends were evidently unable to swing a subsidy, even if they could have had the guns condemned as obsolete.

Simon, Bruni, and others offered the guns in several Latin-American countries in which there were potential customers on both sides of revolutionary fences. There was also considerable discussion of a sale to Benito Mussolini, to whom Coster personally had a solid pipeline. Italy, technically a non-belligerent although openly backing the Franco rebels in Spain, was eligible to buy the Lee-Enfields. Whether Il Duce intended to give or sell his potential rifle armament to the Falangists or whether he had more remunerative plans elsewhere, Coster didn't know and didn't care. Coster did know that Spaniards were killing Spaniards on the Ebro, on the approaches to the Alcazar in Toledo, on the fringes of Madrid where the Loyalists were holed up in University City, and that rifles were in demand. As long as he could collect, he cared little for the "fifth column," as Ernest Hemingway called it. He would sell to anybody in Spain or elsewhere who needed a few hundred thousand tried and true rifles (well, fairly true—whether the Lee-Enfield rifles were as accurate at 2,000 yards as the American Springfield has never been properly adjudicated) and the Devil take the hindmost.

Alfred Shrigley of Boston, a former Mexican consul, recalled being approached on the subject of rifles being available in wholesale lots below the Rio Grande. "I was told," he said, "that any number of Lee-Enfield rifles were available to be sold anywhere, and that they were being stored in large quantities in Connecticut. When I asked if forty or fifty thousand were available, I was told that they were, and more if I wanted. The price was twenty-two or twenty-three dollars a rifle. At any rate, the Mexican government was not interested in the proposition."

When his fair-haired boys proved unable to put over a deal that seemed to him to be a gift of the gods on a silver platter, Coster moved into the negotiations personally. He made the terrifying trip to New York City on numerous occasions to confer with foreign agents who were probably just as terrified but for completely different reasons. At such cloak-and-dagger meetings, he was known only as Doctor Müller.

Arrangements for payment for the rifles were worked out

in detail. At one stage of the negotiations, Coster discussed matters wtih Lewis A. Shea, then executive vice president of the First National Bank of Bridgeport, Connecticut. The bank, which was not involved in the original financing of the deal, was merely asked to provide a banking service—the handling of drafts on New York City banks to cover the rifle sales. Funds for the purchase of the guns were to be on deposit in New York City banks, and as deliveries were made, money was to be transferred to Bridgeport for contract performance. Although attorneys for the bank scoffed at the plan because (they believed) there were no rifles available outside of government arsenals, they insisted that the contract contain a stipulation that the bank's services be contingent upon the rifles being withdrawn from government warehouses with full government authority.

The stipulation amendment was sent to Wingersky for Coster's signature. There is no record of the signed agreement ever being returned to the Bridgeport bank.

Whether any of the two million-odd rifles were ever sold remains at this late date a matter of conjecture. Many of Coster's associates are convinced that the boy from Mulberry Bend—with or without the benefit of orthodox banking channels—made his usual killing. Just who was killed—there was a unanimity of legend that some of the guns had finally been sold to a revolutionary or counter-revolutionary group in one of the more politically volatile republics of this hemisphere—will probably never be known. Even the New England bankers were not sure of what had actually taken place. But it is a matter of record that one of them remarked to a colleague, one of the wealthiest men in the area: "Next time that bird at McKesson & Robbins has something else exciting planned, be sure to get in touch with me."

The multimillion-dollar venture into gunrunning, whether or not it ever came off, was probably the most secret of all of Coster's bizarre machinations, and one of the most impressive to the few who knew about it. Once again the insiders were dazzled by the Great Man's enterprise and imagination. Among other things, this fling into international intrigue lent greater credence to the legend of his intimate contacts with Very Important People throughout the world.

No doubt about it: F. Donald Coster was a man to follow.

14 : First Shadows

THE MIDDLE '30's were F. Donald Coster's golden years. His empire was strong and prosperous. McKesson & Robbins' sixty-six outposts reached into thirty-five states and Hawaii. The firm was nationally recognized as one of the three largest in the drug field. Its 1937 gross income from wholesale distribution of pharmaceuticals and liquor, together with the manufacture of drugs, cosmetics, and distilled liquors, totaled more than $174,000,000. Net profit passed the $3,500,000 mark, and inventories were valued at more than $44,000,000. Other assets gave the company a total net worth of some $88,000,000.

Of this strong and prosperous empire, Coster was cock of the walk, king of the hill, top dog. He was not only president; he was the company. His board of directors was a round table of puppets that moved only when he pulled the strings. Hard-headed financiers and big businessmen, they had been brought to heel by the impact of his driving ambition, the brilliance of his ideas, and, of course, the fat dividends on their investments. They had followed him blindly, happily, and obediently as he expanded his sprawling domain. They had no reason to be suspicious of the nonexistent fleets of the crude-drug division plying the oceans of the world with their nonexistent cargoes, as long as McKesson & Robbins, Ltd., the Canadian subsidiary, reflected fabulous profits on the books of the company.

Socially Coster had achieved all the status he was ready to acknowledge. He entertained senators, governors and bank presidents aboard his yacht. His wife's chows won cups and ribbons in the best dog shows. He was invited by P. Hal Sims to serve as honorary referee in Sims's famous 150-rubber bridge match against Ely Culbertson at the Regency Club— a flattering gesture, for although Coster liked to play bridge, his colleagues did not accept his self-appraisal as an expert; in fact, they regarded him as a duffer.

He had achieved status as a philanthropist. In 1934 he put up $2,000 to help his Fairfield employees start a credit union that in two years had accumulated a fund of $20,000 to invest. In 1935 he sponsored the Fairfield Free Heart Clinic "to provide medical and surgical care, treatment and medication to indigent applicants, regardless of race, creed, sex, or age." Rooms were taken in the Medical Building at 881 Lafayette Street, Bridgeport. Dr. Marcus Backer, leading heart specialist in the area, contributed his services, as did Dr. Clifton C. Taylor, pediatrician, who acted as consultant in children's cases. Miss Margaret Murray, a registered nurse, completed the staff. Although Coster financed the annual budget of $2,500, the clinic was actually Carol Coster's favorite project.

As a public gesture of his fraternal devotion to Freemasonry, Coster donated forty acres of land in Bethel, Connecticut, to the Masonic Cemetery Association, Inc., a nonstock corporation founded "to provide a fraternal and charitable cemetery." Coster poured $35,000 of his own money into beautifying the place, building a four-foot field-stone wall and planting the rolling hills with flowering dog-woods and rose beds. The name was later changed to Bethel Memorial Park Association.

One of the most satisfying moments of his career came in 1937 when he received, okayed, and returned the proofs of the biographical sketch that was to appear in Volume XX, the 1938-39 edition of *Who's Who in America*. (He over-looked the omission of an *e* in the spelling of *Schieffelin,* the new maiden name he had given his wife.) His reaction must have been a glowing one such as every fiction writer feels when he sees his work in type for the first time. The para-graph read:

> **COSTER, Frank Donald,** corpn. official; *b.* Washington, D.C., May 12, 1884; *s.* Frank Donald and Marie (Girard) C.; Ph.D., U. of Heidelberg, 1909, M.D., 1911; *m.* Carol Jenkins Schiefflin, of Jamaica, L.I., N.Y., May 1, 1921. Practicing physician, N.Y. City; 1912-14; pres. Girard & Co., Inc. (succession to Girard Chem. Co.), 1914-26; pres. McKesson & Robbins, drug mfrs., since 1926; also pres. McKesson & Robbins, Ltd.; dir. Bridge-port City Trust Co., Fairfield (Conn.) Trust Co. Methodist. *Clubs:* New York Yacht, Bankers, Lotos, Advertising (New York); University, Black Rock Yacht (Bridgeport); Brooklawn Country. *Home:* Fairfield, Conn. *Office:* McKesson & Rob-bins, Inc., Bridgeport, Conn.

Coster was no longer the lean and hungry challenger; he was the fat and arrogant champion. Yet he was still a man—and afraid.

It is difficult to understand why a man who was a Prussian tyrant to his underlings—and even to his colleagues—a man who walked among chemists with post-graduate degrees brazenly posing as a Heidelberg alumnus, should be so terri-fied of strangers. True, the genuine Heidelbergers were not very frightening characters. Most of them were like Dr. Emil Fanto—whose brains Coster had been picking since the

Girard & Co. days—mousy, unworldly scientists who would not have dared challenge the boss even if they had been suspicious of him. Dr. Fanto himself was a wispy little man scarcely five feet tall, weighing not much more than a hundred pounds, who, though he still spoke with a strong German accent, apparently did not find it strange that Coster, a Ph.D. from Heidelberg, never addressed him in German.

Strangers, however, were always a potential source of danger. The lengths to which the Costers went to protect their privacy could be exemplified by the Ostermoor incident. Carol Coster wanted some specially designed cushions made for the afterdeck furniture of the *Carolita*. Since the Ostermoor Company, one of the country's leading manufacturers of mattresses, was located only a few miles away in Bridgeport, Coster summoned its experts.

Normally a firm the size of Ostermoor wouldn't be bothered by so small a project as yacht cushions, but in deference to Coster's prestige and his proximity, Ostermoor agreed to oblige.

Louis Lebowitz, vice president of the firm, promised to bring samples of materials to Fairfield personally. Ruth Krupka, daughter of the president of Ostermoor and a textile stylist in her own right, selected a number of fabrics and decided to go along with Lebowitz to present them. They drove to Coster's home, parked, and walked to the house together.

The butler who answered the door courteously but firmly refused entrance to Miss Krupka. Dr. and Mrs. Coster, he explained, were expecting only Mr. Lebowitz, and the young lady could not be admitted.

"But Miss Krupka is the daughter of our president," Lebowitz protested. "She is a textile designer. It is she who has selected the patterns for the *Carolita*'s cushions."

The butler was sorry, but he had his instructions. The master's orders were inviolable. The young lady would have to wait in the car.

Unaccustomed to such cavalier treatment—and, of course, unaware of Coster's phobia about strangers—Miss Krupka stalked fuming back to the car where she sat for the hour it took for Carol to choose a fabric worthy of the Coster bottoms.

Business was too good. When men who have shared a storm-tossed adventure find themselves in the calm waters of an apparently safe harbor, they become bored. To Coster, with his burden of guilty secrets and his fear of exposure, the smooth sailing was only an illusion, and he grew more and more arrogant, growling and snapping at such trusted associates as Julian Thompson. Even the polished Thompson himself became restive.

Thompson was coauthor of the Coster Miracle. He had fought the battles to consolidate the positions his "discovery" had blueprinted. Now that the tooth-and-nail stages had been passed, the treasurer of McKesson & Robbins had leisure to exercise his responsibility of examining the fiscal relationships between the various divisions and the over-all operation as represented by the Maryland holding company.

Checking over his reports in early 1937, Thompson seriously pondered the isolated position of McKesson & Robbins, Ltd., the Canadian subsidiary. Year after year the thriving, worldwide trade in crude drugs showed the best margin of profit of any division of the organization. But Thompson was disturbed by the practice of the Canadian firm of pumping all profits back into the crude-drug trade. The resultant stockpiling of huge inventories made no sense to Thompson.

The most recent figures from Canada showed that warehoused goods and accounts receivable had reached the impressive total of $18,000,000.

Thompson felt that part of the profits should be funneled back into the treasury of the parent company to reduce the outstanding debts. He broached the subject to Coster. His recommendation was brusquely rejected by the president.

"Do you consider it good business to hobble the most thriving division of the company?" Coster demanded. He went on to point out that withdrawing funds from the crude-drug division would mean curtailing its activities and reducing its profits.

Coster spoke with such an air of finality that Thompson dropped the subject, at least for the moment. He had learned that Coster was never friendly to a new proposal that was not his own, particularly when the proposal concerned his pet project, the Canadian subsidiary for which he took full personal responsibility.

Realizing the futility of pursuing the issue with Coster, Thompson discussed it with some of his fellow directors. They agreed that it was advisable to reduce the crude-drug division's inventory, but how? They were reluctant to attack the problem head on. To avoid the appearance of *lèse majesté,* they decided to approach the problem obliquely. At the next board meeting, therefore, instead of cracking down on the Canadian subsidiary alone, they voted to reduce the inventories of all divisions of the company by $4,000,000, and use the savings to reduce the firm's long-term bank obligations. The crude-drug division's share of the inventory cutting was $1,000,000.

Coster was not pleased by the majority decision but apparently accepted it with good grace.

During the summer of 1937, while Coster was on one of his rare visits to the 44th Street offices in New York, Thompson told him that he was planning to take his family to Poland Springs, Maine, for a vacation.

"While I'm that close to the Canadian border," the treasurer added, "I'd like to visit the Montreal warehouses. No one ever seems to go there and I think someone should."

"Excellent idea," Coster agreed.

No sooner had Thompson reached Poland Springs than he received a telegram from Coster ordering him to report immediately to the Fairfield offices. Leaving his family in Maine, Thompson rushed back to Connecticut, only to be kept cooling his heels for most of the day. When Coster finally received him, he requested him to stay overnight for a conference on financial statements next morning.

When Thompson was finally allowed to return to Poland Springs, he had hardly had time to relax on the broad verandas of the sprawling old nineteenth-century resort when he received another emergency call from Coster asking him to return to Fairfield. Once again he was engaged in a lengthy discussion of the firm's affairs. Thereafter, at intervals of four or five days, Thompson was repeatedly summoned to Fairfield, so that when his vacation ended he had still been unable to visit Canada.

On his return to the New York offices, furious at Coster for interrupting his vacation so often, Thompson reviewed the "emergency" discussions to which he had been called and could find none of them sufficiently important to justify Coster's urgency. With reluctance he finally concluded that the only possible reason for the repeated summons to Fairfield must have been to keep him from visiting Montreal. For the first time in thirteen years Thompson's solid confidence in

Coster began to waver. He had better stop asking questions and start digging out answers.

His first shock came when he discovered that Coster had ignored the vote of the board of directors in the matter of Canadian inventories. Instead of reducing the stock of crude drugs in Montreal warehouses as the board had directed, Coster had increased it by another million dollars. Next, checking through the books, Thompson could find no record of insurance on the multimillion-dollar Canadian inventory. Alarmed by this unorthodox omission, Thompson went to Coster, expecting to be told that the matter was a mistake or an oversight.

Coster blandly explained: "Why, they are insured by W. W. Smith & Co. The Smith people guarantee the accounts, and handle all of the business, including the insurance."

When Thompson questioned the wisdom of such an arrangement, Coster blew up.

"How can you criticize the fine record of the crude-drug division?" he shouted. "Much of the credit for our profitable operation in Canada is due to the Smith firm."

In view of the long and successful association of McKesson & Robbins with W. W. Smith, Thompson had no suspicions about the firm at this time. But he was growing more and more puzzled by the mystery with which Coster surrounded the Canadian operation. Why were only George Dietrich and, to a lesser extent, Robert trusted to share with Coster the secrets of McKesson & Robbins, Ltd.? Why, in fact, were there secrets? Was there anything to hide? As treasurer of McKesson & Robbins, Inc. (Maryland), the parent company, Thompson had previously accepted the reports of the Canadian division as gospel, just as he accepted the figures of the other divisions as normal routine. Coster's strange behavior during his Maine vacation, however, and the curious practice of leaving the insurance of millions of dollars' worth of crude-drug stocks in the hands of a broker, even though it was the reliable W. W. Smith, sent Thompson back to the books for a second look.

He discussed the matter with John McGloon, the comptroller, who confessed that he, too, had been disturbed about the unorthodox situation in the crude-drug division. McGloon said he had questioned Coster about the Canadian firm several months earlier and had been assured that everything was in order. The practice of plowing profits back into inventory, Coster explained, had been adopted because the primary goal of the division was still growth. When McGloon persisted in his questioning, Coster lost his temper and told him that his business was to run the comptroller's office, not to worry about matters of high policy.

McGloon turned over his records to the treasurer for a few days, but Thompson got nothing from them but an increasingly uneasy feeling that something was wrong.

Coster's private intelligence network quickly brought him the news that Thompson and McGloon had been in conference. He summoned the comptroller to his office and cross-examined him at length about his business with the treasurer. He rejected McGloon's explanation that his conversations with Thompson were perfectly normal exchanges of business information such as they had been having for years as officials of the firm.

Coster got up and began to pace the floor.

"You may as well tell the truth," he said. "I know all about the plot."

"What plot?" McGloon's surprise was genuine.

"The plot to get my job." Coster's voice rose in anger.

"There's a conspiracy, and Thompson is the ringleader. He wants to be president of McKesson & Robbins himself. He's been poking his nose into everything around here, giving the impression that he's conducting a secret investigation that will show me up as a bad president."

"I know of no secret investigation," McGloon said, "or of any conspiracy to get you out of the presidency and Thompson in."

Coster sat down again and glared at the comptroller. Then he banged his desk, warned McGloon not to get involved in any funny business, and dismissed him.

When McGloon reported the scene to Thompson, the treasurer decided to take a leaf from Coster's own book. His investigation had not been secret until then, but it would be in the future. And just as devious as Coster's actions seemed to be. He had no suspicion of dishonesty, for he could not believe that Coster would jeopardize his strong position in business by any chicanery. Basically he was disturbed by Coster's arrogant assumption of dictatorial power and by his evasiveness about the Canadian division, but he was also beginning to have some doubts about the president's genius and the infallibility of his judgment.

15 : The Phantom Companies

Early in 1938 Thompson made a startling discovery in the books of McKesson & Robbins of Connecticut, also Coster's personal fief. He found that W. W. Smith's annual fee of $18,000 and its commission of ¾ of 1 percent were both being paid out of the treasury of the Fairfield subsidiary and not out of the profits of the crude-drug trade, which would be standard procedure. These payments amounted to more than $150,000 for 1937 alone. Coming on top of the peculiar insurance arrangement, the fact that the expenses of the Canadian operation were being paid by the Connecticut division made Thompson more determined than ever to get to the bottom of the relationship between Smith and McKesson & Robbins.

Thompson recalled that the company files contained reports on the Smith company by Dun & Bradstreet, the noted business-rating bureau. He saw the reports each year as part of his treasurer's routine, and they had produced a subliminal confidence in a firm about which he personally knew nothing. In view of the efficiency of Coster's espionage system, he was reluctant to ask for the latest report at this time. He wanted to have more than suspicions to go on before he discussed W. W. Smith with Coster.

Needing a trustworthy outsider, Thompson called on Maitland Dwight, a New York attorney who had been his classmate at Princeton. He asked Dwight to request information on the Smith firm from Dun & Bradstreet.

Thompson was flabbergasted by the news Dwight brought back: Dun & Bradstreet had no record of ever furnishing McKesson & Robbins with a report on W. W. Smith & Co.

Obviously the operation of this strange company, charged with the responsibility for the multimillion-dollar crude-drug trade of McKesson & Robbins, would have to be systematically checked. Even though it was only early spring, Thompson had already decided to give up his 1938 vacation and devote the time to the long, searching, and discreet inquiry he was sure would be needed.

Thompson confided his plans to no one except his private secretary, Doris McNeil. Miss McNeil was an idealistic, intelligent youngster just out of Syracuse University. He knew he could count on her discretion, for she regarded Coster with the utmost disdain. She particularly resented Coster's frequent vituperative attacks on her boss. Once, when Coster had stormed out of Thompson's office after a violent tirade, she exclaimed with some vehemence: "How can you stand such uncouth talk from that stupid oaf?"

"Now, now, Doris"—Thompson had chided her, with a small smile—"you can't call him stupid. He has two degrees from Heidelberg."

"I don't believe it"—Miss McNeil sniffed—"I don't believe that man ever saw the inside of a college."

There was no need to caution Doris McNeil to be circumspect, but Thompson briefed her on the situation anyhow.

"If what I suspect is true," he said, "we are sitting on a powder keg. I have enough information to warrant serious suspicion, but there still may be some valid explanation for the unorthodox procedures I have discovered. Coster is such an unusual man that he just might be doing the right thing in a very peculiar way. Many people could be needlessly hurt if the news of my investigation should become known.

"Still, I feel such a strong obligation to so many people that I've got to find out what's going on," he continued. "I helped put this thing together, and my responsibility would be tremendous if anything went wrong. It was my personal recommendation and testimonial that interested many of these people in the first place. I helped sell securities and involved some of my personal friends. Somehow, the things that appear to be happening are so fantastic that I can't believe them. Mr. Coster is too intelligent and too able a man to become involved in anything so weird. "

Thompson's first step was to go to Price, Waterhouse & Co., the auditors who had been handling the McKesson & Robbins account ever since Coster took over. Had he just thought he had seen annual Dun & Bradstreet reports on W. W. Smith, or did such reports actually exist? They did indeed, the auditors replied. George Dietrich sent them over each year. Price, Waterhouse gave Thompson photostat copies of the last two reports, the latest dated February, 1937. They seemed to be the same as the reports Thompson remembered having seen in the McKesson & Robbins file, indicating that W. W. Smith & Co. was three-quarters of a century old, had branches around the world, owned a fleet of ships, and had a net worth of some $7,500,000.

Armed with the photostats, Thompson went to Dun & Bradstreet headquarters, at which he was told the same thing that Maitland Dwight had learned: Dun & Bradstreet in New York had never been asked for a report on W. W. Smith & Co. Neither had its Bridgeport or Montreal offices. The originals of the photostats must be forgeries—good forgeries, but obviously forgeries. Dun & Bradstreet officials pointed out minor discrepancies. The originals must have been devised from old Bradstreet reports, made up before R. G. Dun joined the firm. The style differed slightly from that used by the rating organization during the years allegedly covered by the Smith reports.

Thompson was relieved to find that the five Canadian warehouses, in which millions of dollars worth of crude drugs were reportedly stored, were actually listed in telephone books. However, further inquiry in Montreal disclosed that the offices there were small and saw relatively little activity. The main business of W. W. Smith was transacted in Liverpool, said the Montreal sources.

Thompson was not really surprised, then, when inquiry in Liverpool brought the reply that Montreal was the center of W. W. Smith operations.

Thompson next started tracing the funds that had apparently been shuttling in and out of the McKesson & Robbins (Connecticut) treasury to finance the crude-drug traffic. As W. W. Smith & Co. was unknown in the banking circles of both Liverpool and Montreal, he began following the commission checks George Dietrich signed and paid to the Smith firm. Since these were drawn on the company's account at the Guaranty Trust Company of New York, he asked to see some of the canceled checks that had been issued to W. W. Smith and not yet returned to Fairfield. The endorsements on the checks indicated that the Smith firm had accounts with the Chase National Bank and a New York City branch of the

Royal Bank of Canada. Investigation showed that neither of these accounts was very substantial or very active. Where then had the funds been channeled?

Manning & Co., described as a private bank and another rather nebulous organization, appeared to be the main fiscal agent for W. W. Smith in its crude-drug buying and selling. Before digging into the Manning mystery, however, Thompson felt he had enough facts to face Coster again. He had worked diligently and covertly all summer and fall of 1938, and he had amassed a file of bewildering evidence indicating that if the Canadian subsidiary was not indeed a "hollow shell," it was at least a cover for some devious manipulation of McKesson & Robbins funds. He still found it hard to believe the evidence. It seemed impossible that a man of Coster's brilliance and stature could have indulged in such obvious chicanery. Thompson was convinced that the assets, which appeared nonexistent as far as the Smith firm and the Manning bank were concerned, must be concealed somewhere. His problem was to find them and quietly restore them to the McKesson & Robbins treasury without a scandal that would endanger the company's position.

Coster had been pressing Thompson to support him in a $3,000,000 bond issue he was anxious to float, so he was not surprised when the treasurer called on him at his Fairfield home on Sunday morning, November 27. After discussing the bond issue at length, Thompson veered to the subject of the crude-drug operation. He expressed serious doubts about the reliability of W. W. Smith & Co. and asked specific questions that had arisen from his investigation. Coster brushed Thompson's queries aside, declaring that the whole arrangement was quite simple; he could clear it up in an hour.

"I'll be in New York tomorrow," he said. "Have lunch with me."

As the two men sat alone together in the Longchamps restaurant at the corner of Forty-second Street and Lexington Avenue, Thompson again demanded clarification of the firm's relationship with W. W. Smith.

"You're a persistent devil, aren't you," said Coster with an amused smile.

The smile vanished when Thompson accused him bluntly of concealing important facts about the business.

His face flushed with anger, Coster declared: "You're part of that damned conspiracy! You're all out to get my job! I'm sick and tired of your sly insinuations, of your trying to discredit me with your malicious rumors. Put up or shut up, Thompson. If you think there's something wrong, prove it. You can't!"

"I want to know more about W. W. Smith & Company."

Suddenly Coster hit the nerve center of the treasurer's doubts. He asked pointblank: "Do you actually believe, Thompson, that there are no assets in our crude-drug division?"

Taken somewhat aback by the directness of the question, Thompson replied: "You're too smart not to have assets, but I've got to know what they are and where they are. And I want to know why you are stalling me."

"I was stalling you yesterday." Coster's smile was not entirely successful. "I wanted to smoke you out. There's obviously a conspiracy in the New York office."

"There's a conspiracy, all right," Thompson said, "but it's your assistant treasurer, George Dietrich, who's the conspirator. George won't give me a straight answer. If you can get him to open up the records of the Canadian subsidiary, it would help immensely."

"Our Canadian position is entirely healthy," said Coster. He looked at his watch. "I'm late for an appointment now, but I'll get together the records and documents in the next day or so to prove to you that the operation is solvent."

The two men shook hands, but there was no warmth in their parting. The old relationship had been poisoned forever.

Julian Thompson did not sleep that night. He hoped against hope that George Dietrich would turn out to be the villain of the piece. His long admiration of Coster would not let him doubt the man's honesty. Coster was in a way his own creation. And yet, as he tossed and turned on his pillow, he could not get rid of the fear that he had created a Frankenstein monster.

Early next morning he telephoned the Fairfield office and was told that the president was in bed with tonsilitis. Since the showdown was postponed another day, Thompson put on his hat and coat and left for Brooklyn. The phone book listed the address of W. W. Smith & Co. as 1 Hanson Place.

He was reassured to find that the building housed a branch of the Chase National Bank. Both the Smith firm and Manning & Co. were listed on the lobby directory. Lettered on the door of the office was the name "George Vernard" with the two firms in smaller letters below.

When he entered the two-room suite, he hardly noticed the tiny, four-feet-seven receptionist who greeted him. Eleanora Lochner, as Vernard's secretary for five years, could have told Thompson a great deal more than he was going to get from Vernard. She could have told him that the business of the Smith and Manning companies was no longer being done in that office; that it had been moved to Stamford, Connecticut, because George Vernard drank on the job and was too often too squiffed to be trusted. She could have told him that her boss telephoned George Dietrich in Fairfield almost every day and that they spoke in Italian. The marks on her fingers, she might have explained, were from the blue sealing wax she had to affix to all letters leaving the office addressed to George Dietrich. Finally, she might have told Thompson that George Vernard's real name was Arthur Musica. This she had learned from a petition for separate maintenance filed by his wife, in which it was alleged that her husband ran fictitious companies.

As a postscript, Miss Lochner might have added that her major chore was to make a daily purchase of oysters, raw onions, and lemons—the components of Vernard's favorite hangover remedy.

Ushered into George Vernard's inner office, Thompson got only evasive answers, and the strong effluvia of alcohol wafted across the desk. Vernard was only the New York agent for the Smith and Manning firms. All information must come from the Montreal office.

As soon as Thompson left, Vernard picked up the phone to report the visit to George Dietrich in Fairfield.

Dietrich immediately hurried to 400 Mill Plain Road to bring the bad news to Coster's bedside—and Coster panicked for the first time. The fear that had been haunting him was on his heels; the nightmare was coming true. The ghost of Philip Musica was at the door.

He could not believe that Thompson was acting alone. He must be the spokesman for a conspiracy of directors to oust Coster as president. And there could be no compromise with

Thompson. There was no common ground on which Coster's amorality could meet the Princetonian's unswerving conscience.

The fact that Coster did not know and could not believe that Thompson was acting alone probably saved the treasurer's life. The problem of Thompson alone would have been solved quickly and without qualm or scruple. But fortunately Coster could not believe that Thompson was still holding back, still hoping prayerfully that Coster had an honorable explanation for a seemingly impossible situation. Coster could think only in terms of conspiracy.

Coster accepted the challenge. He left his sickbed and went to the phone. Once again it was the boy from Mulberry Bend against the world—self-preservation and the law of the jungle. There was a possibility that he might still call the turn if he could catch his adversaries by surprise.

Coster made two phone calls that, in effect, planted a time bomb designed to wreck any further investigation by Thompson. The exact details of his complex maneuver are obscure, and efforts to learn them in the months to come were legally blocked.

The first phone call ordered the transfer of 2,000 shares of McKesson & Robbins common stock, held in Mrs. Coster's name, to the name of one Herbert Dietrich, apparently another nonexistent relative, so that when a second transfer was made to implement Coster's scheme, the name Coster need not appear.

The second phone call apparently went to Benjamin Slade of New Haven, one of Connecticut's most astute and experienced lawyers—although Slade later defied a federal grand jury that wanted him to produce letters and documents and answer questions showing his possible connection with Coster. Slade was upheld by federal Judge William Bondy, who ruled that conversations between an attorney and his client were privileged in perpetuity, even if the client had died. In any event, there is little doubt that in those first days of December, 1938, Slade conferred with Mayor Thomas J. Spellacy of Hartford, another topflight lawyer and a power in Connecticut Democratic politics, and that the mayor was asked to suggest some possible surprise legal action that might be taken by a McKesson & Robbins stockholder that would effectively block access to company records by "conspirators."

Back in his sickbed, Coster continued to give orders in a voice so hoarse it was barely audible. He told George Dietrich to remove from the company vaults certain records, canceled checks, and cash. He gave Dietrich two ledgers containing handwritten diaries covering his activities between 1920 and 1938. Dietrich wrapped the ledgers in brown paper, and that night, after he had cleared the vault of possibly incriminating evidence, hid his cache in an abandoned shack on the factory grounds.

If there was to be war, the decks were cleared for action.

After another sleepless night, Julian Thompson telephoned Fairfield again and was told that Coster was still bedridden. Resolved that the showdown should not be postponed a day longer, he took the train for Fairfield and went directly to Mill Plain Road. Coster's throat infection was genuine enough—he could scarcely speak—but Thompson showed him no pity. Without preliminaries, he handed the president the photostats of the so-called Dun & Bradstreet reports on W. W. Smith & Co.

"The Dun & Bradstreet people say these are forgeries," he declared.

Coster sat up in bed. The color drained from his face.

"There must be something wrong here," he said. "Why, W. W. Smith is an old firm. It's everything this report says it is. There must be something wrong at Dun & Bradstreet's."

Silently, Thompson shook his head.

"Thompson," Coster blurted, "just what is it you want?"

"I want to be satisfied about this thing here and now," the treasurer replied. "I want straight answers. I want to know who Manning & Company are. I want to talk to someone from Manning who can tell me about the routine of payments. I want the privilege of going into our Canadian warehouses and checking the inventories."

"The inventories are there all right," Coster said. "I can assure you that the affairs of our crude-drug division are in perfect order. Why don't you write out a list of questions——?"

"I insist on being allowed to see for myself," Thompson interrupted.

Coster glared at the man whose admiration and backing had been his passport to respectability and fortune, the man who was now his enemy.

"If you refuse to take my word," he croaked, "you are calling me a liar. That's enough. I demand your resignation as treasurer . . . immediately . . . before you leave this house."

"I have no intention of resigning, Mr. Coster," Thompson said, "until I find out whether or not this company I've helped to build is being run on the level."

Coster sank back on his pillows and shook a warning finger at his treasurer.

"If you do anything to wreck the credit of McKesson & Robbins, Thompson, you'll regret it. If you don't stop this nonsense, I'll throw the company into receivership and wipe out the common stockholders."

Thompson gasped. Was Coster losing his mind? He himself held about 10 percent of the common stock—some 105,-000 shares—and virtually no preferred.

"You're the one who'd suffer the most, Mr. Coster," he said. "You're the largest common stockholder."

"Get out of here," said Coster.

That did it. Although Thompson gave himself the rest of the week to think it over, he knew there was only one answer. He had taken a viper to his bosom and he must tear it out. The genius he had discovered, the financial wizard he had praised and promoted, the brilliant and imaginative business tycoon he had admired, was apparently no more than an uncommon rogue. He would have to be destroyed.

On Monday, December 5, 1938, Thompson called Coster in Fairfield and told him that he was bringing the results of his investigation to the attention of the McKesson & Robbins executive committee at the earliest possible moment.

Coster croaked a hoarse acknowledgment and hung up.

16 : The Unraveling

W<small>HILE</small> Julian Thompson was telephoning from New York, the time bomb Coster had set ticking the previous week exploded more than a hundred miles away in Hartford, Connecticut. A stockholder named Vincent W. Dennis filed an equity receivership action against McKesson & Robbins.

Actually, Dennis had been a stockholder only a few hours. The 2,000 shares of common stock in his name had been transferred from Mrs. Coster's account through the intermediary of the phantom "Herbert Dietrich." Dennis was the corporation counsel for the City of Hartford and his action was part of Mayor Spellacy's response to Benjamin Slade's request for a scheme to protect McKesson & Robbins' credit by tying up company records until a matter of $20,000,000 in missing assets could be cleared up.

Attorney Walfrid G. Lundborg, representing Dennis, said the purpose of the action was to preserve the assets of the corporation and to effect a reorganization. Dennis' affidavit charged mismanagement and waste.

Federal Judge Edwin S. Thomas immediately appointed

two receivers: Mayor Thomas J. Spellacy of Hartford, and Attorney Abraham S. Weisman of New Haven. Late that Monday afternoon Weisman left for Fairfield, where he had the combinations changed on the McKesson & Robbins safes and vault. He did not know that George Dietrich, on Coster's orders, had already removed many incriminating records.

When news of the receivership reached Wilbur L. Cummings, a partner in the law firm of Sullivan & Cromwell, which represented McKesson & Robbins, he immediately started calling fellow members of the drug company's executive committee, all of whom were members of the board of directors. One of them, Sidney J. Weinberg, a governor of the New York Stock Exchange and a partner in the investment banking house of Goldman, Sachs, suggested meeting in his apartment in the Sherry-Netherland Hotel. Cummings telephoned Thompson (who had already heard the news), William J. Murray, Jr., first vice president, and Charles F. Michaels, executive vice president of McKesson & Robbins.

Of the five men meeting at the Weinberg apartment at nine o'clock that evening, four were disturbed and puzzled by the news from Hartford. The fifth, Julian Thompson, had a story to tell that shocked them far more than the news of the receivership. Obviously under great tension, he told them how his suspicions of the crude-drug division had led him into the maze of strange relationships between the firm and the Smith and Manning companies. They listened in dismay as he told them of the forged Dun & Bradstreet reports and his fears that the inventories in Canadian warehouses might be nonexistent. They were speechless when he estimated that more than $20,000,000 might be involved.

Thompson pointed out that he had hesitated to bring his

suspicions into the open until he had given Coster every opportunity to explain the peculiarities of the situation. He said that his high regard for Coster's ability and intelligence made it difficult for him to believe that the firm's president could engage in what appeared to be a flagrant swindle. He repeated that Coster had always operated secretly, particularly in his international trading in crude drugs, so it was still possible that Coster was engaged in some business negotiation that he was not yet ready to disclose. Thompson's listeners expressed fervent hopes that there might be some such honest explanation of the mystery.

Weinberg put in a call to Fairfield, even though earlier attempts to reach Coster had failed. He got through immediately.

Coster feigned great surprise. "What receivership?" he exclaimed.

Weinberg told him.

"I know nothing about it. Surely somebody could have told me, living right here in Connecticut."

"This is a frightful thing," Weinberg said. "I think you ought to come to New York as soon as possible to meet with the executive committee."

Coster promised to come in at ten o'clock the next morning.

When Weinberg reported Coster's denial of any knowledge of the receivership, Thompson laughed bitterly. He told his colleagues of his angry argument with Coster the previous week, and of Coster's threat to throw the company into receivership if Thompson didn't "stop this nonsense." It was obvious to all of them that Coster must be behind the receivership petition in Hartford. The receivers would impound the company's records, thus halting Thompson's investigation and giving Coster time to find a way out of his troubled predicament. The directors reasoned that Thompson's threat to inform the executive committee of his suspicions had triggered Coster's actions. Testimony at later hearings proved their assumption to be correct.

Round One, apparently, was Coster's.

But the executive committee was not going to take Coster's gambit passively. Before the meeting at the Sherry-Netherland broke up, Cummings called Washington and woke up William O. Douglas, chairman of the Securities and Exchange Commission (who was to be appointed to the United States Supreme Court the following year). Would the S.E.C. investigate possible fraudulent statements in connection with McKesson & Robbins stock offerings? Douglas promised immediate action.

Weinberg then got George May, senior partner of Price, Waterhouse, out of bed, and induced him to dress and come to the hotel. May was greatly worried by developments, in view of the auditing firm's long association with Coster, but he assured the executive committee that the McKesson & Robbins books were in order.

Weinberg then called John M. Hancock, chairman of the stock-list committee of the New York Stock Exchange, telling him about the receivership and the consternation of the executive committee about the crude-drug division. Weinberg asked Hancock to take steps to halt trading in McKesson & Robbins stock next morning so that all stockholders might be given equal protection.

Rumors of the receivership had been circulating in Wall Street before the market opened on Tuesday, December 6. Promptly then, at the 10:00 A.M. opening, there were selling orders for 1100 shares of McKesson & Robbins stock, normally a slow mover, at the market. (At the previous closing, only 200 shares of common had changed hands at 7½ and 400 shares of preferred had been traded at 36½.)

The market orders were never executed. At 11:30 A.M., the governors of the New York Stock Exchange suspended trading in McKesson & Robbins securities. Officials of the Exchange emphasized that they had ordered the suspension not because of anything they knew but because of things they did not know. The stock-list committee wired company executives in New York and Fairfield a formal request for full information.

After the suspension of trading on the Big Board, dealings in McKesson & Robbins stock moved to the over-the-counter market. On that first day, common closed at 5 bid, 5½ asked; preferred at 28 bid, 32 asked; and bonds at 100½. The range on McKesson & Robbins securities in 1938 prior to the suspension had been: common, 9¼ to 5⅜; preferred, 41 to 27. Quite obviously, the early news of the receivership and suspension caused no panic dumping.

Coster, however, had anticipated panic selling and had taken steps to salvage some of his personal capital in case his receivership action should provoke disaster in Wall Street. Bernard Abramson, securities accountant in the New York attorney general's office, testified later that several days before equity receivership proceedings had begun in Hartford, trading in McKesson & Robbins shares had been quite brisk. There was heavy selling for the account of Carol Jenkins Coster, probably without her knowledge, recording a paper loss of some $40,000. On the same day, Carol's brother John O. Jenkins was also getting rid of his holdings. Although only 400 shares were recorded as sold in his name, his account with Steiner, Rouse & Co. showed a balance, when trading was suspended, of 10,000 fewer shares than it had contained several days earlier.

Coster had the colossal nerve, five days before trading was halted—and just about the time he was plotting his receivership action, which he knew would throw Wall Street into a state of palpitation and cold sweat—to request permission from the stock-list committee for the listing of additional McKesson & Robbins convertible debentures due in 1950 (twenty-year bonds bearing 5½ percent interest) plus more than 54,000 additional shares of common stock. The committee took no action.

On the morning that trading was stopped, the executive committee of McKesson & Robbins sat in the Manhattan offices on East Forty-fourth Street, anxiously awaiting Coster. Ten o'clock passed—without his promised appearance. Weinberg looked at his watch every few minutes. Thompson consulted the New Haven railroad timetable for the next trains. At last the phone rang.

It was Coster, calling from Fairfield. It would be impossible for him to come to New York, he said. The receivers had ordered him to stay put.

It was a busy Tuesday for all hands. The New York office of the Securities and Exchange Commission began a complete investigation of McKesson & Robbins. The temporary receivers in Hartford issued a public announcement emphasizing that the receivership in no way reflected on the solvency of the corporation. This was supported by a statement by Michaels, the executive vice president, after the executive committee meeting. He said:

> The receivers have satisfied themselves of the solvency of the company. . . .

The crude-drug department of the company is the only department involved. The extent to which the assets of [this] department is involved will not be known until an investigation is completed. [This division] is quite unrelated to the principal business of the company, and there appears to be no question of the company's solvency and continuance in business. All departments, except that involved, have been advised to continue business as usual.

Meanwhile, Julian Thompson had organized a counterattack against Coster's guerrilla tactics. Two days later (December 8), as soon as Frederic Wingersky, head of McKesson & Robbins' legal department, questioned the legality of the appointment of the receivers in Hartford, Thompson and his truth-seeking colleagues filed a petition in federal court in New York for reorganization under Chapter X of the Chandler Act. The petition, adopted by the board of directors and signed by Michaels, stated that "information has come to light within the last few days indicating that the inventories and accounts receivable relating to the crude-drug business have been grossly overstated for a substantial period and the current purported position of the petitioner [McKesson & Robbins] as appears on the balance sheet is false and misleading."

Federal Judge Alfred C. Coxe in New York granted the petition and appointed William J. Wardall trustee and Michaels assistant trustee. As the Chandler Act proceedings took precedence, Mayor Spellacy in Hartford then requested dissolution of the temporary receivership there. Judge Thomas granted the request, thus destroying Coster's plan to use the receivership as a screen to cloak his desperate search for loopholes.

Round Two was Thompson's.

As McKesson & Robbins was the first major corporation to enter reorganization under Chapter X of the Chandler Act, the legal profession was watching closely for possible precedents. Chapter X called for appointment of an independent trustee who had no previous connection with the company. The trustee had three specific responsibilities. First, he was to prepare a reorganization plan acceptable to the creditors, the stockholders, Judge Coxe, and the Securities and Exchange Commission. Second, he was to run the business without interference by the stockholders as long as the firm remained in reorganization. Finally, he was to recover all missing assets. According to the petition, these were estimated at $10,000,000, a figure that would still leave the company solvent, for the balance sheet of October 31, 1938, listed assets of $86,500,000 and liabilities of $76,250,000.

Judge Coxe knew Wardall's reputation as an expert in corporate reorganization and had appointed him only after a long conference in his chambers. Still, Wardall's responsibilities placed him in an extremely peculiar position. Realizing the special nature of the business, he decided he must retain key executives to keep the company going. Nine of these essential executives were also members of Coster's board of directors, in which capacity they had voted to pay dividends that may have been illegal. As stockholders, they had also shared in these dividends and were thus vulnerable to possible legal action on two counts. These directors pointed out that they had been enticed into the great merger by fraudulent statements. Their lawyers declared that they had traded the assets of their respected and solvent family firms for what now were, apparently, fictitious assets of McKesson & Robbins and that therefore they were injured parties with grounds for suit against the firm. Wardall indeed considered these men to have been Coster's victims. He was also worried that they might pull out of McKesson & Robbins to form a competitive group. So he did his best to induce the nine to remain at their posts, all the while dickering with them to return some of their questionable profits to the corporation treasury.

On Friday, December 9, New York Supreme Court Justice Aaron Steuer signed an order tying up cash and securities valued at some $100,000 in Coster's brokerage account for possible future restitution to the McKesson & Robbins treasury. Next day Judge Steuer signed a similar order freezing the brokerage account of Carol Coster, which was of about the same amount. Mrs. Coster's account was tied up at the instigation of New York Attorney General John J. Bennett, Jr., in order to check the possibility that she held funds derived from fraudulent activity by her husband. There is no evidence to indicate that Mrs. Coster knew how much money was in her account, let alone how it was acquired. So long as her charge accounts were unlimited, her chows continued to win blue ribbons, her exclusive yachting parties aboard the *Carolita* were considered status symbols, and her pet philanthropy, the Fairfield Free Heart Clinic, attracted favorable notice, Carol Coster was apparently uncritical of the business life of the man she called "Daddy."

As the McKesson & Robbins scandal continued to make front-page headlines from coast to coast, an army of investigators rushed to get into the act. Ambitious young prosecutors and detectives representing eight federal, state, and local agencies raced each other knee-deep in the rising tide of printer's ink. Uncle Sam was involved in six of the probes, New York state in one and New York City in another. The inquiries were produced and projected with all of the fanfare and press pageantry of the opening of the highly competitive Broadway season. Among the stars and sponsors were:

1.) New York's District Attorney Thomas E. Dewey, lusting for the governorship of New York state—and the presidency—who saw political hay in the field if grand larceny in New York County were involved. His men were digging up grounds for grand jury proceedings.

2.) United States Attorney General Homer Cummings assigned the case to his protégé and star assistant, Brien McMahon, who was later to become an illustrious United States Senator acclaimed as the "Father of Atomic Energy." He also assigned Attorney Thomas Dodd, who was to succeed to McMahon's Senate seat and achieve national prominence in his own right some years after McMahon's death. Cummings, McMahon and Dodd were all from Connecticut, the setting of the Coster drama.

3.) The U.S. postal authorities were seeking to determine if McKesson & Robbins used the mails to defraud. They were amazed when they discovered that a great part of the voluminous "foreign" correspondence was hand-delivered from Robert to George Dietrich.

4.) The Securities and Exchange Commission, determined to protect the stockholders, was endeavoring to discover the extent of the fraud and the whereabouts of the "assets" of the fictitious crude-drug division of Coster's firm.

5.) The United States Bureau of Internal Revenue conducted a sweeping investigation into the company's income tax payments. Tax deficiencies against the firm were being claimed for 1931 when the government claimed that a $195,000 payment had been made instead of the $272,000 due.

6.) Agents of the alcohol unit of the U.S. Treasury were

checking the books of the company seeking possible violations of the alcohol tax act.

7.) The U.S. Department of Agriculture had its analysts checking the products of the company to determine whether they were up to government-set standards.

8.) State Attorney General John J. Bennett was conducting public hearings with witnesses from the executive offices of the company in New York.

During a hearing conducted by Assistant Attorney General Ambrose V. McCall in New York City, the manager of Price, Waterhouse, Albert B. Ritts, explained the position of his auditing firm in regard to the McKesson & Robbins account. Ritts' estimate of the "alleged loss" was $18,000,000, of which $10,000,000 was inventory and $8,000,000 accounts receivable. Ritts said that accountants from his firm had never visited the Canadian warehouses in which the crude drugs were supposed to be stored, but that all the warehouses had been asked for statements of supplies on hand. The confirmations were checked against the records in the Fairfield offices of McKesson & Robbins, and even the postal cancellations of the replies were checked to make sure the letters originated in the towns listed as sites of the warehouses.

As for on-the-spot checking by auditors, Ritts said: "After all, they could show me a barrel of crude drugs and say it was this or that, and I wouldn't know one from the other."

He insisted that most of the companies recorded as doing business with McKesson & Robbins, Ltd., were "among the most reliable in the British Empire" in the crude-drug field. He admitted he had been taken in by the forged Dun & Bradstreet reports on W. W. Smith & Co., who had been paid fees and commissions amounting to $154,000 in 1937. When Mc-

Call commented that the Smith firm had been paid for doing nothing, Ritts nodded and said soberly:

"It looks that way."

Following Ritts in the witness chair was Geoffrey G. Row-bottom, a Price, Waterhouse partner. He testified that his company had been preparing annual audits for Coster as far back as 1925, first for Girard & Co. and later for McKesson & Robins, on the basis of a formal letter of instructions signed by Coster. The last letter, dated December 8, 1937, was read into the record. It provided for a balance-sheet examination of the parent company and its subsidiaries and a general review of the profit-and-loss account. One paragraph in the letter of instructions illuminated Coster's technique for deceit: it specifically excluded a detailed check of cash and other bookkeeping transactions.

The Price, Waterhouse fee was $75,000 a year, plus $17,000 for expenses. Rowbottom pointed out that because of the many divisions of McKesson & Robins, the audit required looking into the books of practically eighty-five different companies. Like everyone else, he was stunned by the implications of the testimony, particularly by the statement made the previous day by A. D. Whiteside, president of Dun & Bradstreet, that the reports on W. W. Smith & Co., which Price, Waterhouse had accepted as gospel, were forgeries.

"I can't bring myself to believe that the whole thing is nonexistent," Rowbottom said. "There must be assets someplace, but where I couldn't tell you. An entire letter-writing plant would have been necessary to transact the alleged sales and to mail statements to our firm from warehouses concerning stocks of crude drugs on hand—if this had been done fraudulently."

Rowbottom did not know then how close he was to the

truth. While he was testifying, Joseph F. Ruggieri was in Montreal investigating for New York Attorney General Bennett—and reporting that the Canadian "warehouses" were nothing more than telephone numbers and mail drops.

At the same moment Robert Galp, an agent for the Securities and Exchange Commission, was unearthing the "letter-writing plant" that Rowbottom skeptically had predicted would have had to exist. Galp found a McKesson & Robbins chauffeur who said he often drove Robert Dietrich from Fairfield to Stamford, Connecticut. Galp went over the trail and discovered that Dietrich always stopped at a Stamford bank. The bank proved to be a dead end, but in the bank building he struck pay dirt.

Offices over the bank, Galp found, had been vacated only a few days before. Most of the furnishings had been removed, but in the drawer of an abandoned desk, he found a strip of wrapping paper that had been used as a liner. The wrapper had once held a package addressed to George Vernard, and bore the return address of a New York City printer.

Galp located the printer who told him he had been printing letterheads for Coster for years. The details of his instructions were most enlightening. All paper used had to be of British manufacture and watermarked. The letterheads bore the names of several British firms, and each one had to be printed on paper of a different texture and watermark. Invoices and receipts were also printed at the same shop, bearing the names of corporations all over the world, all of them prominent in the records of McKesson & Robbins' crude-drug trade.

Galp reported his findings to James J. Caffrey, regional administrator of the Securities and Exchange Commission, who immediately cabled Scotland Yard. Ten hours later the answer came back: none of the British firms whose names appeared on the letterheads had any record of transactions with McKesson & Robbins.

Further investigation disclosed that the Stamford "letter-writing plant" had been staffed by a lone stenographer. Her name was Rose Otting, and she had originally been employed by George Vernard in the Brooklyn office of Manning & Co. When Coster decided that Vernard's drinking had become a security risk, he moved the operation—and Miss Otting—to Stamford, where it could be more easily supervised from nearby Fairfield. Vernard and his bottles were left behind with a friend recommended by Miss Otting, Eleanora Lochner.

Miss Otting left Brooklyn before Vernard had reached his onions-and-oysters stage of alcoholism, and she knew none of the guilty secrets Vernard had unwittingly revealed to her successor while in his cups. Miss Otting was convinced that she was doing important secretarial work for an international business network. She had every reason to be impressed by its importance, for few secretaries have had so much equipment. Miss Otting did her work on a battery of seven different typewriters, each with its distinctive type face. One of her major responsibilities was to make sure that each typewriter was mated with its own set of stationery and business forms. She was cautioned again and again that W. W. Smith, Manning, and the five Canadian warehouses must never never be confused with a typewriter other than that matched with its letterhead. Miss Otting typed all correspondence, trading orders, and inventory statements as instructed by Robert Dietrich.

Robert would take Miss Otting's output back to his brother George in Fairfield. It was there treated as though it had come from Canada, the nonexistent canceled stamps ostensibly going into George Dietrich's imaginary stamp collection. The fictional sales, purchases, bank deposits, and withdrawal reports were fed into the McKesson & Robbins accounting department as factual data.

While Galp was uncovering the Stamford "letter-writing plant," Joseph Ruggieri was reporting from Canada to New York Attorney General Bennett. He had found that A. H. Raymond & Co., one of the putative warehouses, was only one room in the pretentious Dominion Square office building in Montreal. Staffed by a public stenographer named Mrs. Bessie Waldon, it was merely a mailing address. Mrs. Waldon said she had been hired five years earlier by two men she had never seen before and was paid $6 a week. Her services consisted of receiving one or two letters a month and forwarding them to A. H. Raymond & Co. at 1 Hanson Place, Brooklyn, N.Y.

Ruggieri also discovered that E. E. Pierson & Co., another "warehouse," was also just a mailing address—a desk in a typewriter sales office manned by one Everett Smith. Smith's salary was $7.50 a month and was paid, as was Mrs. Waldon's, by Violet Quesnot, who was in charge of the two-room Manning & Co. office at 1396 St. Catherine Street. Miss Quesnot had been hired nine years earlier by George Vernard. Her job was to forward all mail unopened to his Brooklyn office.

Miss Quesnot was also charged with setting up and staffing the mail drops that were the blinds for warehouse addresses. Since it was difficult to keep people interested in the dull routine of remailing letters, particularly at such low pay, she had a rather high turnover, and finding replacements was her most difficult job. At first all mail was turned over to her for forwarding to Vernard, but she was later told to have the agents readdress mail directly to Vernard at 1 Hanson Place, Brooklyn. Miss Quesnot, in her supervisory capacity, was the highest salaried member of the Canadian staff. She was paid $27 a week.

Miss Quesnot was also in charge of the W. W. Smith & Co. office, located a short distance away in the Medico-Dental Building at 1405 Bishop Street. She staffed this office with a teen-age girl named Betty Whyte who got $7 a week. Miss Whyte's most exacting duty was sitting in for Miss Quesnot during lunch hour.

After hearing Miss Quesnot's story, Ruggieri asked the Royal Canadian Police to check the addresses of the supposed warehouses in Toronto and Ottawa. These, too, were found to be nothing more than mail drops. There were no warehouses, no multimillion-dollar inventories of crude drugs shipped from the far corners of the earth. Just as Julian Thompson had feared, McKesson & Robbins, Ltd., was nothing more than a "hollow shell." And Julian Thompson's discovery and protégé, the genius from Heidelberg who knew more about the drug markets of the world than any other living being, was nothing more than a grandiose mountebank.

The next step was automatic. The board of directors of McKesson & Robbins met in special session at the New York offices on December 12 and passed a resolution calling for the resignation of F. Donald Coster as president and George Dietrich as assistant treasurer. The two men were also asked to resign as directors.

Julian Thompson, sick at heart, insisted that the board meet again a week later—to take further action in case the resignations were not forthcoming.

17 : Point of No Return

WHEN the directors asked Coster to resign as president of McKesson & Robbins, they were unwittingly asking him to sign the death warrant of the character he had created with such care over the years. F. Donald Coster and the president of McKesson & Robbins were one character. Separate them and, like Siamese twins, one or both would die. He could not possibly have resigned.

His inner reaction to the request for his resignation must be left to students of the subconscious. What is known is that he made no reply to the board of directors in New York. Instead he wrote a formal letter of resignation from the board of directors of the Bridgeport-City Trust Company. Although Coster had been a director of the bank for several years, he had never attended a meeting of the board. Some of these men were also on the McKesson & Robbins board, and were also his backers in his original deal to acquire the venerable drug house. He was obviously making a Freudian substitution. He could not submit his resignation to a board containing his betrayer, Julian Thompson; he was bowing to men who perhaps still believed in his genius. The document, dated December 13, 1938, was simple. It read:

> I hereby resign as a director of the Bridgeport-City Trust Company, such resignation to take effect immediately.
>
> (signed) F. Donald Coster

Coster realized he had reached the point of no return. His hitherto nimble brain had been searching fruitlessly for a way out of his dilemma. The proud dreadnought he had created to fight his way into the closed circles of the big drug monopolies was awash with scandal, on the verge of foundering. He still stood steadfastly on the bridge, but the enemy guns of blame and shame were trained on him. His panic-stricken erstwhile colleagues were scurrying from the ship, rushing from hearing to hearing to cry out their dismay and disclaimers of guilt. There was a carnival air in the hearing rooms as the public and private defenders of the law fought for page-one space in the next edition of the newspapers. Everyone was groping for the truth, but only he knew it. He also knew something that no one else seemed to understand—that he had built so well, had made the House of McKesson & Robbins so basically strong that it would survive the fears and panic of his old admirers now scurrying for cover.

Aside from submitting his resignation to the Bridgeport-City Trust Company instead of to his own board, Coster made the only other move he had considered since the receivership action was instituted in Hartford. He retained Samuel Reich, an outstanding Connecticut lawyer, as his counsel.

It was high time. On December 13, Hector Dowd, agent for the Securities and Exchange Commission, asked for the arrest of F. Donald Coster, George Dietrich, and George Vernard on charges of filing false information with the commission. United States Commissioner Garrett W. Cotter issued the warrant. But the magic of F. Donald Coster, the industrial titan, was still strong medicine. He was not forced to come to the law; the law would come to him. He was still ill at home. It was no longer a matter of mere laryngitis. He was under the care of a Bridgeport psychiatrist, Dr. Daniel P. Griffin, so he was excused from coming to New York to be arrested. Instead, he would submit to arrest in Fairfield. It was agreed that George Dietrich would also submit to arrest in the Coster home.

So Coster waited for the law to bury him and resurrect Philip Musica, the boy from Mulberry Bend. It was a curious twist on the Robert Louis Stevenson morality tale of *The Strange Case of Dr. Jekyll and Mr. Hyde*. In the Stevenson classic, when the good Dr. Jekyll became definitively the horrid Mr. Hyde, he could no longer resume his gentler incarnation. In the current version, the horrid Mr. Musica had become the great and good Dr. Coster, and he would be publicly poured back into the mold of the nasty little swindler and stool pigeon of Elmira and the Tombs. It was a chilling prospect.

The federal officials came to Mill Plain Road in Fairfield on Wednesday morning, December 14. They were preceded by Samuel Reich, Coster's attorney, who arrived at exactly nine o'clock. A few minutes later Assistant U.S. District Attorney Irving R. Kaufman arrived from New York, followed at nine-thirty by U.S. Commissioner Robert M. Alcorn, U.S. Attorney Arthur T. Gorman, and U.S. Marshals Bernard Fitch and Stephen Lopresti. Sometime during the interim George Dietrich had entered the house alone by a back door. They assembled in the library.

At exactly 9:32 A.M., F. Donald Coster made his dramatic entrance. For the first time the great bright star of Bridgeport's industry was on stage before such an audience. In addition to the principals, twenty reporters and photographers crowded into the library. I was one of them, covering the story for the Bridgeport *Sunday Herald*. As a local reporter there was something eerie about the scene to me. I was struck by the recollection of the years when this man's privacy was so sacrosanct that he was able to refuse interviews, drive photographers away, and scorn the wrath of the editors. After all, he had served on boards of directors with the publishers, who bowed like the rest to his whims and arrogance. Now he was being treated like a common criminal, completely vulnerable to the public spotlight. The tragedy and drama of the moment were evident in the stricken, blind look that glazed his eyes. He seemed unaware of the spectators to his disgrace. Dressed in a brown bathrobe over a white shirt with black tie and black trousers, he stood hesitantly in the doorway leaning on the arm of Dr. Griffin, his psychiatrist. After a brief pause, Dr. Griffin dropped his arm and with a soft pat on the shoulder sent Coster into the room.

The library was a sunny corner room with large windows, and was lined with bookcases. There were many pictures both on the walls and in profusion on small tables. A large portrait photograph of Theodore Roosevelt dominated one wall, and a painting of the *Carolita* steaming through heavy seas hung on another. A framed photograph of Mrs. Coster stood on one table next to a framed motto which read: "When you get into a tight place and everything goes against you till it seems as if you couldn't hold on a minute longer, never give up then, for that is just the place and time the tide will turn. —Harriet Beecher Stowe." Many of the smaller photographs were of familiar American and foreign statesmen. There were also several family groups, some of them Orientals.

Coster stalked past George Dietrich who, with a dazed look on his face, sat in a straight-back chair. He gave his brother not the slightest glance as he slumped into a padded leather chair directly under the portrait of Theodore Roosevelt. His elbow rested on the top of his desk, and he cupped his chin in one hand during most of the procedure. He was obviously under great strain and just as obviously determined not to show it.

As Commissioner Alcorn opened the hearing, Coster's attorney, Samuel Reich, arose to declare that his clients would waive reading of the warrants. U.S. Marshal Fitch then took the warrants and turned to Dietrich, saying: "You are under arrest."

George Dietrich remained as silently motionless as a statue.

Fitch then turned to Coster, who still sat with his chin in his hand. "Mr. Coster," he said, "you are now formally under arrest."

Coster, too, sat as if in a trance. His only reaction was to raise his heavy-rimmed glasses and pass his hand over his eyes.

Commissioner Alcorn set bond at $5,000 each. Reich asked that his clients be released in his custody until bail could be supplied by a bonding company later that day.

Kaufman agreed. He also waived the question of removal from the state when Reich, speaking for his clients, agreed that they would appear in the federal court for the Southern District of New York whenever summoned to answer charges of violating Section 32 of the Securities Act of 1934: filing false financial information with the Securities and Exchange Commission. The offense was punishable by up to two years in prison or a $10,000 fine or both.

The entire proceedings took only fourteen minutes. A bond application was handed to Dietrich, who signed automatically, hardly glancing at the papers. Coster read his through slowly before affixing his signature with a pen borrowed from a newsman. There was a brief moment of silence, broken by an announcement by Attorney Reich that the business was concluded.

"No, no, that's not all," broke in Marshal Lopresti, nervously patting his fingerprinting equipment. Kaufman then turned to Reich and told him his clients would have to be fingerprinted.

Coster was obviously upset. He spoke in an undertone to his attorney, and Reich, after speaking to Kaufman, then led Coster and Dietrich into another room for a conference that lasted several minutes before the lawyer summoned the federal officers, and Lopresti proceeded to fingerprint the accused out of sight of reporters and photographers.

While his inky fingers were being rolled one by one against the card, Coster said irritably, "This is pesty." Apparently he had no fear that the prints could be compared with the official records of his past. He was convinced that the last traces of Philip Musica had definitely disappeared from the files of police and prosecutor as a result of the looting expedition he had engineered in 1929.

When Lopresti had completed his chore and Coster and Dietrich had washed the ink from their hands, the entire party returned to the library. Pictures were taken, after an agreement with Reich that the press would leave the premises immediately afterward. Coster, Dietrich, and their attorney posed until Reich, noting that the tension was mounting in his clients, called a halt.

*　　*　　*

Coster might not have been so confident about the anonymity of his fingerprints if he had known what was going
on in New York City that day. The first step in the unmasking of the boy from Mulberry Bend was taken in the office
of the attorney general for the state of New York. When the
photographs of F. Donald Coster, the drug company executive under fire, appeared in the newspapers of December 11,
Henry Unterweiser, an investigator for the state attorney general since 1910, thought they looked familiar. Unterweiser
bought all the papers he could lay his hands on and compared
the various pictures with the images filed in his memory. It
wasn't long before he made the connection: Coster was the
man he had known as William Johnson when they had
worked together investigating German espionage during the
first months after the entry of the United States into World
War I.

Unterweiser reported his suspicions to his superiors and
described "Johnson's" previous criminal record under the
name of Philip Musica. The possibility that Coster might be
Musica was a breathtaking development, but none of the
higher-ups in the office could remember back to 1917, and
a rush to the records was disappointing. The dusty files
yielded only one set of fingerprints labeled Philip Musica,
and that was too blurred to be compared to any that might
be made of Coster. Further search brought another surprise:
somehow, some time, the voluminous dossier labeled "Philip
Musica" had disappeared from the attorney general's office.

Several veteran newsmen also noted a resemblance of Coster to old pictures of the Italian immigrant's son who had
masterminded the cheese fraud of 1909 and the human-hair
swindle of 1913, and they questioned New York's Assistant
Attorney General McCall about it. McCall was cautious, so

long as there was no documentary proof. There was a remote possibility that the physical resemblance might be a remarkable coincidence. A false identification of a man of Coster's position with a background substantiated by the highly respected *Who's Who in America* would be disastrous. McCall would only say: "There is considerable doubt as to Coster's identity. I have reason to believe that Coster is known to this office under a different identity."

When reporters pressed him for amplification of his statement, McCall had no further comment. In view of official silence and the impressive stature of the harassed drug tycoon, even the boldest tabloids were circumspect.

On the same day of Unterweiser's tentative identification, however, James J. Caffery, regional administrator for the Securities and Exchange Commission, received a phone call from a man in a nearby city who said he could produce the real name of Dr. F. Donald Coster. Caffery sent an agent to interview the caller, who showed him an old, yellowed bill of lading, keeping his thumb over the lower right-hand corner.

"Under my thumb," said the man, "is Coster's real name and signature, but I'm afraid to show it to you. It might cost me my life."

A fraction of an inch below the handwritten signature hidden by the man's thumb, the agent was able to read a typewritten name.

"Okay," said the agent casually, "if that's the way you feel about it, we don't want your information." And he hurried back to his office to report to Caffery that the name was Philip Musica.

Caffery called Washington and discovered that there were no prints on file for Philip Musica. He checked with the New

York police and found a grizzled old desk sergeant who remembered the name Musica and the hair swindle. But when
he checked further, he ran into the same consternation that
had rocked the attorney general's office: the Musica files had
disappeared!

On Thursday, December 15, the attorney general's office
obtained a set of Coster's prints from U.S. Attorney Kaufman, who had brought them back from Fairfield. Comparison
with the smudged Musica prints, however, was impossible.
That afternoon the Coster prints were turned over to the
bureau of identification of the New York police department,
where a frantic search was still going on for the missing Musica files.

Hope was fading with the early winter twilight when
Inspector James J. Donovan, chief of the bureau of criminal
identification, suddenly remembered that duplicate files of
some old cases had been stored in the Sheriff Street station
house on the lower East Side. He immediately dispatched a
crew to dig into the ancient records.

Far into the night Donovan's men delved into the dust
and cobwebs of New York's criminal past. They turned up
the dossiers of half-forgotten crimes: Albert Patrick, who
killed William Marsh Rice, the Texas oil millionaire; Dr.
Waite, the poisoner of Riverside Drive; the Benedetto Mon-
dania case, that broke the power of the Black Hand over
Little Italy. Packet after dusty packet piled up on the floor—
but still none bearing the name of Philip Musica.

At last, after six backbreaking hours, a grimy detective
came up with a folder of yellowing documents—the Musica
file! They were all there—the records of the bribery of customs officials in 1909, the human-hair swindle of 1913, the
subornation of perjury of 1921 that grew out of the "poultry

trust" murder of Barnet Baff. And particularly there was a fine, unblurred, well-preserved set of fingerprints.

The prints were rushed to headquarters where Inspector Donovan was waiting with the card brought down from Fairfield. The two sets matched perfectly to the last loop and whorl!

Shortly before midnight on December 15, Inspector Donovan summoned the press to Centre Street. He told newsmen that Dr. F. Donald Coster, the financial wizard and president of the vast McKesson & Robbins pharmaceutical empire, and Philip Musica, the twice-guilty swindler from Mulberry Bend, were one and the same person.

While Donovan was giving the story to the press, Coster was seated in his library in Fairfield with Samuel and Philip Reich, his attorneys. Since nine o'clock that evening the lawyers had been listening while Coster proudly led them back over the parade route of his past. He gloried in the development of McKesson & Robbins under his presidency. His main theme was the depth of his dedication to the company.

"This has been my life," he said. "If they take it from me, they take my life. I don't care about the money. I never did. I wanted only to create a great company and see it grow into a greater one. Without my planning, my work and my sacrifices, it would never have survived the Depression. I had to do many things to save it, particularly when it was losing money. I had to make it show a profit. Now it is strong, and it will continue to be one of the strongest organizations in the world."

It was one o'clock in the morning of Friday, December 16, when the Reich brothers took their leave of Coster. In New York City the newspapers were grinding out the story of his amazing masquerade for a million breakfast tables, and the wire services were telling it to millions more from coast to coast. In his study in Fairfield, Coster pulled paper from a drawer in his desk and sat down to write his own version of the McKesson & Robbins story.

As he wrote, the family pattern once again emerged. Once again, as he had when the cheese fraud and the hair swindle had collapsed, he took full responsibility upon himself, absolving his brothers, his wife, and his brothers-in-law from any wrongdoing. As for himself, he had done nothing for personal gain or aggrandizement. His every act had been one of devotion to the company.

The night was close to an end when he wrote his final line, sealed the message in an envelope addressed to Samuel Reich, and went upstairs for a few hours of troubled sleep.

After Wednesday, when the federal officers had come to arrest and fingerprint her husband, Carol Coster was on the verge of a nervous collapse. She was frantic about what Coster might do, and with reason. George Dietrich had told her that Coster had said he would kill himself if he lost the company.

Secretly she searched the house for firearms. She found three revolvers. She put each in a separate bag and enclosed the lot in a zipper bag that she furtively gave to Willy Richartz, the butler, with whispered instructions to give them to William Williamson, the gardener, to hide. Williamson took the guns to his apartment over the garage and hid them on a shelf in his closet.

During the day Mrs. Coster managed a word with the gardener while she was looking after her dogs. "Get rid of those guns," she said. "He knows they're gone and he's been looking all over for them."

Williamson hid one gun in the tool shed and put the other two in flowerpots on the shelf under the stairs leading to his apartment. Shortly thereafter he saw Coster enter the garage and start rummaging through the cars and in the tool kits. He took off immediately on an imaginary errand. Knowing Coster's hypnotic power, he was afraid he would not be able to lie convincingly if his employer asked him where the guns were.

When he returned, the gardener found that the revolvers under the stairs were gone. He reported the loss to Mrs. Coster, who then instructed the butler to get rid of all the bullets he could find in the house. From then on, she vowed that her husband would never be left alone if she could help it.

The next day, Thursday, was the butler's day off, so she brought Williamson into the house as his substitute. The gardener was not very good at buttling, but he could keep a watchful eye on Coster. Williamson remembered overhearing Mrs. Coster pleading with her husband to give up the revolvers.

"Please, Daddy. Please give them to me. I'm so frightened."

"Don't be silly, Carol darling. You don't think I'd be foolish enough to use them on myself, do you?"

"Then why don't you give them to me?"

"Because I need them." Coster's voice rose in anger. "If that two-faced Thompson ever has the nerve to come back here, I want to be armed when I meet him."

"Oh, Daddy, please. That would only make matters worse. Please be calm. Please don't do anything rash. Promise."

"I promise."

"Then give me the guns. Please."

Coster bristled. "I've promised, haven't I? Isn't my word enough?" And he stalked away.

The next morning, Friday, December 16, the morning after his nocturnal session with the Reich brothers and his committing to paper of his own version of the McKesson & Robbins story, Coster awoke at 7:30 A.M. The cold light of a December morning filtered through his window as he slipped into his bathrobe. In the pocket of the bathrobe was one of the revolvers he had retrieved from the garage. As he came downstairs for breakfast, he was followed closely by Leonard Jenkins, one of Mrs. Coster's brothers, who had been assigned to guard duty for that day.

Coster breakfasted on orange juice and coffee, refusing anything else with a wordless shake of his head. Jenkins sat across from him, eating his own copious breakfast, occasionally trying to interest Coster in food. No cereal? No toast? No eggs? No bacon? Coster rejected them all with another silent headshake. For an hour he sat there without speaking, lost in the enormous silence of his mind. Then, with a suddenness that startled Jenkins, he slapped his hand on the table and asked for a highball.

When Jenkins brought him the drink, Coster drained half of it in one long swallow, and got up from the table. Carrying his glass, from which he took occasional sips, he began to wander through the downstairs rooms of the villa on Mill Plain Road. He paused occasionally to touch a chair or a table, looking about him with a bemused expression. Once he stopped for a long admiring look at the portrait of Theodore Roosevelt, probably remembering the day, hardly a year past, when he had been asked to run for the Republican nomination for President of the United States.

"Another drink, Leonard."

Jenkins complied nervously. He knew that Coster rarely took more than one or two drinks—never before the sun was over the yardarm—and here he was on his second at ten o'clock in the morning.

Upstairs, Mrs. Coster was still asleep. She had been awake most of the night, listening for small noises, worrying about her husband, crying silently in the darkness. She had finally succumbed to exhaustion. Coster looked in on her several times, moving carefully to avoid waking her. Each time he found her in a deep sleep.

"Another highball, Leonard."

Despite his libations, Coster walked and talked with complete coordination. He examined the V.I.P. photos of which he was so proud and made comments Jenkins did not understand. He fed the tropical fish. He told Jenkins how he had broken the quinine trust in Java and Holland and the iodine trust in Chile—stories Jenkins had heard many times before.

At about ten minutes before noon the telephone shattered the oppressive quiet of the house like an alarm bell. Coster started, then picked up the phone. The call was from George Dietrich's house. George had been taken into federal custody and the federal officers were now on their way to pick up Coster.

The president of McKesson & Robbins—he had still not resigned and the executive committee would not act on his failure to resign until the following Monday—gently replaced the instrument in its cradle. He stood up.

"Another highball, Leonard," he said.

Again he revisited briefly the glories of 400 Mill Plain Road, a house which his neighbors regarded as just another plush suburban villa but which to Coster had been a palace. Highball in hand, he started up the stairs.

Jenkins followed, halted on the landing when he saw his brother-in-law go into the bathroom and close the door, then went back downstairs. A few minutes later he remembered his assignment and retraced his steps.

"Are you all right?" he asked at the bathroom door.

"Yes, I'm all right," Coster replied. "I'll be out in a few minutes."

Reassured, Jenkins went downstairs again.

From the bathroom window, Coster could see the entire length of his driveway. As he watched, two cars drove up. The first one stopped in front of the house and George Dietrich stepped out, followed by United States Attorney Arthur Gorman and United States Marshals Fitch and Lopresti. Attorney Philip Reich was alone in the second car. At the end of the driveway Coster's favorite pet, a massively handsome Saint Bernard chained to his doghouse, barked wildly as the men approached the front door.

Carol Coster had awakened, had emerged yawning from her bedroom. Coster could hear the heels of her feathered mules clicking in the hallway.

Coster moved away from the window and turned to face his reflection in the medicine-chest mirror. What he thought of at that instant, nobody will ever know. Does anybody ever know what a man thinks of at the moment of truth? Did he think of Mama Assunta, the roly-poly genius of his poverty-stricken amoral youth, who had passed on to him her shrewdness, her driving ambition, her egocentric ruthlessness? Did he think of her superb homemade ravioli and gnocchi, her Gargantuan laughter, her indomitable will? Did he think of his ineffectual father who would rather have remained honest had it not been for Assunta? Did he regret the Teutonic masquerade that had forced him to deny his Italian heritage to such an extent that he was overjoyed when his chauffeur Frank Verilli would bring him some of his Aunt Madaloni's lasagna? Did he at last look at his image in the mirror and see himself as the boy from Mulberry Bend whom he had thought he had destroyed forever and who was now looking at him reproachfully from the nonexistent world beyond the glass?

Coster drew the revolver from his bathrobe pocket and raised it to his head.

Downstairs on the porch Marshal Lopresti rang the front doorbell. As though on cue, Coster's finger squeezed the trigger. The jangle of the bell was lost in the shattering blast of gunfire and the scream of Carol Coster.

The federal officers wrenched open the door and rushed into the house. Jenkins was racing up the stairs. The officers were close behind. As they reached the landing they saw him smash his way into the bathroom, splintering the door around the lock.

Jenkins stood for a moment as though paralyzed, blocking the doorway. The horror-stricken officers peering over his shoulder saw Coster lying on his back in the bathtub, his legs dangling over the side. The force of the bullet, fired into his right ear, had spun him around. His eyeglasses, unbroken, had fallen into the wash basin. A .38 caliber police-positive revolver lay on the floor.

It was nine minutes past noon, Friday, December 16, 1938.

18 : "As God Is My Judge . . . "

I HAD ARRIVED at Mill Plain Road a few minutes after twelve. About thirty reporters, mostly from New York newspapers and other out-of-town publications, were clustered at the end of the driveway. Police Chief Arthur Bennett was standing in front of the house awaiting the arrival of the federal officers. Using the prerogative of a local newsman and an old and close friend of the chief, I ignored the others and walked through the crowd to join him. A colorful police officer, he had fared well over the years in my news stories of adventures and activities and he needed little persuasion to give me the advantage. I wanted to be in the house when Coster was taken into custody. At Bennett's suggestion, we walked around to the rear of the house and entered through the back door. The other reporters had clearly taken little notice of my arrival. The out-of-towners perhaps believed I was just another member of Bennett's police force. The few local boys must have had something else on their minds. At any rate it was fortunate timing for me.

Once we were inside the house Bennett left me to my own devices, warning me not to get in the way. I headed for the library remembering the wealth of pictures scattered around that room. Moving about practically on tiptoe, in harmony with the heavy silence in the house, I snatched photographs from the various tables. Vaguely I heard the sound of cars coming up the drive and then the chattering of reporters' voices demanding to be admitted to the house. I walked to the library doorway to watch for their entrance.

A moment later, three sharp sounds in staccato sequence split the quiet of the house: the ring of a doorbell, the blast of gunfire, the scream of an anguished woman. Coster's suicide shot was like the starting signal for pandemonium.

There was a feeling of unreality about the scene as I saw several men burst through the door and rush up the stairs seemingly in pursuit of Jenkins. It was as though some stage director in the wings was trying to create an aura of bedlam.

As I headed for the stairs, Attorney Reich, his eyes wide with disbelief, came down and passed me as though I were not there. I turned to watch him for a moment. He walked to the doorway facing the newspapermen gathered on the porch and said, "Get a doctor, quick!" Then with the jerky motion of an automaton, he raised his right arm, put his forefinger against his temple, and said "Boom!"

I dashed up the stairs and joined the group standing in front of the splintered bathroom door to share with them the hushed shock of the macabre ending to a magnificent masquerade. Dr. F. Donald Coster, the great entrepreneur of the McKesson & Robbins empire, was a crumpled corpse lying on his back in a bathtub, dead by his own hand. He had remained president of the company to the end. Having refused to resign, he had beaten the deadline for his ouster, set by his former associates determined to change him back to Philip Musica of Mulberry Bend.

Chief Bennett's voice cut through the silence. "All right men. Now you've seen it. Everybody downstairs." The group turned and followed his orders. I walked along with Bennett. As we passed the entry to the upstairs sunroom, we saw Carol Coster lying on the floor, her head cradled in her brother's arms, her body rocking with anguish. She moaned, "Somebody told me Donald just shot himself." Then she screamed, "My God, Daddy, why did you do it? Why did you do it? Why didn't you face it? My God!" Her body relaxed evidently in another faint.

Chief Bennett went into a bedroom and called for the police ambulance. I waited for him and we went downstairs together. In the brief interim, Jenkins had revived his sister and helped her down to the first floor where he placed her on a chaise longue in an alcove off the living room. A maid took over and cared for her mistress. Nearby on a divan, George Dietrich sat alone. Tears streamed down his cheeks as he murmured over and over again, "Why did he do it? Why did he do it?" It was the same shocked query that had burst from Carol's lips only moments earlier. Dietrich seemed on the verge of collapse.

A few minutes later, the police ambulance arrived. In spite of the tenseness of the atmosphere, I had a moment of humorous relief when the door opened and Police Sergeant Thomas Murphy came in carrying the front end of a stretcher. The man on the other end was Al Baum, a reporter from the Bridgeport *Times-Star* who was also covering the story for the New York *Daily News*. The moment the door had closed in the faces of the other reporters, Baum dropped

Questioned by prosecuting attorneys, Vernard admitted that he was a brother of Coster and the two Dietrichs. He was formally charged with giving false and misleading information to the Securities and Exchange Commission, and arraigned before federal Judge William Bondy. Special District Attorney Gregory Noonan requested that bond be set at $100,000, citing the past record of the Musicas as fugitives from justice. Attorney Milton Hertz, attorney for Vernard, raised no objection to the high bail, but reserved the right to seek a reduction at any time. Vernard was taken to the Federal House of Detention and lodged in a cell not far from those already occupied by his brothers, George and Robert Dietrich.

For his action in holding Leonard Jenkins and the two Coster servants overnight while he was checking fingerprints, Fairfield Police Chief Arthur Bennett was accused of unnecessarily highhanded treatment of the three men. But, as it developed, placing these three men physically in jail served a useful purpose in the wild post-mortem period as far as the effect on the public was concerned. Coster had created such a local legend as a mystery man, that his death set off a chain reaction of fantastic rumors. Some gossips were sure that Coster had fled to safety and that the suicide story was merely an invention to cover up official complicity in his escape. Other gossips were convinced that he had been murdered.

The magic of Coster's personality overcame all logic and all evidence. The day before Coster sealed his unspoken confession with a bullet in his brain, the Bridgeport *Telegram,* a morning paper, expressed an editorial caution to its readers to observe the presumption of innocence. In its edition of

December 15, 1938, in an editorial headed RESERVE YOUR
JUDGMENT, the *Telegram* said:

> Let's be fair about it.
>
> The American public is fond of boasting about its spirit of
> fair play. Now is a good time to show it.
>
> Two prominent citizens of the communities of Bridgeport
> and Fairfield have been placed under arrest by orders of the
> Securities and Exchange Commission in connection with the
> crude-drug assets of McKesson & Robbins.
>
> We'll admit that on the surface the facts look "fantastic," to
> quote the word of the treasurer of the company as given to the
> Stock Exchange committee which conducted the investigation.
> We'll admit that the disclosures have shocked everybody. But
> isn't it true that if amazement is followed by anger, anger is
> apt to be followed by a sort of mental lynching party in which
> the victims are not allowed to say a word in their own defense?
>
> So far as these communities knew anything about F. Donald
> Coster and George Dietrich up to the time of these disclosures,
> they were good citizens, good in their relationships with their
> communities and with their neighbors, vital factors in the
> building up of a big industry which they brought to Fairfield
> and which has distributed millions of dollars in payrolls to
> thousands of persons in this vicinity. The company is a going
> concern. It is still a going concern and its ability to do busi-
> ness is unimpaired even by these disclosures.
>
> Now as to Messrs. Coster and Dietrich. Neither of them thus
> far has said a word in his own defense. The whole story is go-
> ing to come out. We are going to know not only what was done
> but why it was done and what the object was. In the common
> spirit of fair play we ought to withhold judgment until all the
> facts are in, then form our judgment on the whole picture and
> not just part of it. We may have a different feeling when all
> is known.

Release of the text of Coster's suicide note gave most people "the whole picture," but not all. Even twenty-five years

later there are veteran McKesson & Robbins employees who are not entirely convinced that the official version of his death was true. From time to time, the story of Coster's "being seen living a life of luxury" in Italy or South America is revived, despite the fact that his body was reposing in a local undertaker's parlor over the weekend following his suicide.

The funeral home was owned by John Shaughnessy, brother of one of the local policemen who had worked on the case. The Shaughnessys achieved considerable prestige as authorities on the authenticity of the corpse. John himself became a celebrity in his own right as he screened the "very important people" who wanted to view and verify the identity of the remains. There was never any doubt in the minds of Coster's associates who made the dismal visit to Shaughnessy's funeral parlor, yet the dramatic doubt still crops up periodically.

"As God is my judge, I am the victim of Wall Street plunder and blackmail in a struggle for honest existence. Oh, merciful God, bring the truth to light."

With these words, Coster had ended the suicide note written in the lonely hours of his last night of life. Most of the message, addressed to Samuel Reich, his attorney, was devoted to a scathing denunciation of his colleagues, although he refrained from identifying them by name. The only names he used were those of his brothers and brothers-in-law, whom he absolved from any wrongdoing. He also declared categorically that his "poor loving wife was ignorant" of what had been going on in corporate circles.

The principal purpose of the document seemed to be the vindication of Coster's operations, and a reiteration of his selfless dedication to the company. Coster acknowledged he had inflated profit reports in the Depression years of 1930 to 1932, but only to save the firm from disaster. This stratagem, he insisted, was the only thing that had kept McKesson & Robbins out of receivership at that time.

"In the main," he wrote, "they were wash sales to create a profit that did not exist, and what is missing is the alleged profits, plus expenses and blackmail money paid to maintain it."

Although the note was generally coherent, there was a macabre thread of "last mile" hysteria running through it, a definite awareness of the imminence of unwelcome death.

"My poor wife is the innocent victim of my frantic operations to hold up this concern of McKesson's. My brothers-in-law, Leonard and John Jenkins, did as I asked them because they thought it was right and proper to do so and trusted me. They received no material reward. George and Robert Dietrich took orders."

Coster then tried to justify the creation of his phantom firms, W. W. Smith and the Manning bank:

"If profits hadn't been maintained since 1929, the bankers and lawyers who wanted to milk the company through receivership would have succeeded. I tried to stop them. Let the world judge if the bankers, lawyers, auditors, and appraisers who got millions out of the company knew nothing. The wholesale division in ten years failed to do its part in selling our manufactured products at any profit to the plant. I have not tried to ruin the company or the stockholders. If I did, I could have sold my holdings in 1928 for $3,000,000. Instead, I am a ruined man through the treachery of legal intrigue. The rest of the directors, who are now running for cover . . . were totally unfit to serve as directors. One in particular, now co-trustee, was selling his common stock and that of his friends to the public with full knowledge of the situation under investigation. In my case, I was making a desperate effort to salvage something out of the wreck."

Cotrustee Charles F. Michaels, who was to succeed Coster as president of McKesson & Robbins, was charged by Coster with having sold 15,000 shares of stock owned by himself and his family after learning of the fraud but before it was reported to the Securities and Exchange Commission. At a subsequent hearing, Michaels was able to prove that the sale of his stock had been made before there was any inkling of wrongdoing in the operation of the company. He also produced correspondence with Coster relating to the sale of his stock. Coster had not only approved of Michaels' plan to sell, but apparently even suggested a broker to handle the transaction.

Coster's farewell note made only fleeting reference to his Prohibition years' traffic in pharmaceutical products attractive to big bootleggers. Although he did not mention alcohol, his meaning was clear when he wrote: "If selling nonbeverage cosmetic and perfume preparations up to 1927 was criminal, every large drug house did the same, and the government checked and approved the transactions." This was a truly cursory dismissal of an aspect of his McKesson & Robbins' business that was, in the early years, one of its major sources of profits as it had been for the Girard company.

In retrospect, it would appear that Coster's major blunder was his impulsive decision to throw the company into receivership. Some lawyers suggest that he was trying to keep control of the situation through a friendly receiver. His political connections made it possible for him to move swiftly on this. It seems clear that his strongest motivation was the fear that his colleagues were joined in a conspiracy to unmask and unseat him. He must have believed that he was racing them to the bankruptcy court. The erosion of his steel nerves that had previously withstood years of strain, of subterfuge and concealment, was apparent in his final blast at Thompson and his colleagues: "All of a sudden the treasurer and inside shooters started a secret investigation . . . and ran to cover, making me and my underlings the goats and bringing shame and humiliation to my poor loving wife who was ignorant of the conditions."

Coster's last words were like gospel to those who still wanted to believe in him. Attorney Samuel Reich's comment was typical:

> No one can read that message from the grave and, having read it, not know that Donald Coster has been crucified and destroyed and mercilessly vilified in the name of exaggeration and sensationalism. He died because of consuming unrealized ambition to make his company great.

He then quoted: "The nature of all men is so formed that they see and discriminate in the affairs of others much better than in their own."

The suicide note was not the only message left by Coster. Four other letters, obviously written during the last few days of his life, were found in the house. Reich turned them all over to the federal authorities except one addressed to Mrs. Coster. This, he declared as her counsel, was "personal property."

The other letters contained little more than what Coster had written in his suicide note. All emphasized the innocence of his brothers. One made a sentimental reference to his experience as head of Girard & Co. before he plunged into big business. "I was happy and contented in Mount Vernon," he wrote. "Then I had the ambition to build up McKesson & Robbins for myself and stockholders."

Had he known, or found it possible to believe, that Thompson had not already exposed him to the others, Coster still might have contrived some solution to his dilemma. His associates held him in high esteem, and his mesmeric eloquence might have saved the day had he not jumped the gun on Thompson. But somewhere along the last mile he became bewildered and frightened. He had lost confidence in his own magic. He became the catalyst of his own disaster.

His last letters cleared up much of the mystery of the receivership action in Hartford. He stated specifically that the 2,000 shares of stock Attorney Benjamin Slade of New Haven registered in the name of Vincent Dennis of Hartford to start the equity receivership action had come from Mrs. Coster's account. He explained:

> My wife was in Florida when the account of Stein-Rouse was opened. I simply wanted to make her a gift with which she could make a little for her maintenance in case anything happened to me. The money came out of the Jenkins account which I ordered him to pay over to his sister. This amount originally given to Jenkins was my money realized from the sale of McKesson stock and the balance after paying off my loans, plus profit.

Coster's will, drawn on March 11, 1937, more than a year and a half before his death, made his wife sole heir to all his property, real and personal. It also named her as executrix.

On Monday morning, December 19, 1938, Carol Coster and the two Dietrich brothers stood with bowed heads as Dr. Albert E. Beebe, pastor of the First Methodist Church in Bridgeport, conducted private services for Coster in the Fairchild Mortuary Chapel in Brooklyn. The two brothers, become again George and Robert Musica, wore handcuffs.

An hour later professional pallbearers carried the ornate coffin across the sleet-swept road to a mausoleum in Brooklyn's Cyprus Hills Cemetery. The mourners ascended by elevator to the second floor, where Dr. Beebe read from the Scriptures as the coffin was slid into a crypt. Mrs. Coster had ordered an inscription cut into the face of the crypt:

F. DONALD COSTER

1884-1938

This was her husband. Philip Musica was a complete stranger.

19 : Medalie for the Defense

THE BULLET F. Donald Coster fired into his brain raised coast-to-coast echoes of consternation and chaos. The revelation that the "profitable" crude-drug operation was a multimillion-dollar myth caused nation-wide dismay. The shocking disclosure that the erudite and fascinating business genius who went under the name Dr. F. Donald Coster, with two degrees from Heidelberg University, was instead an unschooled, two-time loser from the slums of New York's Lower East Side had violent repercussions in the sixty-six cities of thirty-five states with McKesson & Robbins branches. In innumerable other cities where retail druggists had been induced to purchase McKesson & Robbins stock, the reaction was close to panic.

The quick action of the New York Stock Exchange in suspending trading in the company shares prevented an immediate stampede. But after a day or two of recovery from the stunning blow, the stockholders rushed to the over-the-counter market. Day after day the prices dropped. Common stock, quoted at 7½ the day before the ban on floor trading was imposed, dropped to a dismal fifty cents a share. Preferred shares and bonds were similarly affected.

The common stockholders were the chief sufferers from Coster's personal disaster. Included in this panicky, fright-stricken herd of dumpers at the market were some of the keen-est executives and financiers associated with the company, men who should have known better, men who took stagger-ing losses instead of buying McKesson & Robbins at the ridic-ulously low figure that, even writing off the false profits of the Canadian subsidiary, they should have known in no way represented the true position of the firm. Wild stories circu-lated widely. Coster's stillborn deal in surplus rifles was in-flated into allegations of his having financed foreign wars, engaged in cloak-and-dagger liaisons with heads of foreign states and mysterious revolutionaries about to overthrow the heads of foreign states as well as having participated in sin-ister cartels involved in international traffic in narcotics. Al-though such stories of his international villainy were later proved to be fabrications, they smeared the prestige of the company he had headed. Its reputation was further damaged by the disclosure of the forged Dun & Bradstreet reports. As the hydra-headed investigations developed, with local, state, and federal agencies and prosecutors fighting for front-page attention, the headlines became more and more sensational.

This was the situation that faced William J. Wardall, the court-appointed trustee, when he took over Coster's desk in the New York office. When the board of directors elected Ex-ecutive Vice President Charles F. Michaels as president to suc-ceed Coster, Michaels resigned as cotrustee, leaving sole re-sponsibility for reorganization to Wardall. Wardall's first thought was to restore public confidence in the company, no mean task in view of the vociferous claims of thousands of creditors and the threats of several organized committees of stockholders who wanted to sue the firm. Wardall resisted all pressures seeking action against the directors who had voted (and accepted) dividends that could possibly be proved illegal. Convinced that protecting the company's reputation was his primary concern, he decided it would be better public relations to seek restitution from these men privately.

"I am more interested in assets than arrests," declared Wardall in a news release. "I am interested in protecting the creditors and some fifteen thousand stockholders, and in conserving the jobs of some seventy-five hundred loyal and honest employees. The sensational criminal charges against certain officers have tended to obscure the important fact that the main organization of the company is sound and its principal service to the public is essential. That service is the wholesale distribution to retail stores throughout the nation not only of its own products, but also of drugs and other products manufactured by some forty-five hundred other companies."

Wardall placed particular emphasis on the fact that despite the scandal, current business strongly proved that manufacturers, wholesalers, retail druggists, and the public had continuing faith in the company. Actually, the firm's sales in the month following the receivership action lagged less than 4 percent behind the figures for the same month of the previous year. The fundamental health of McKesson & Robbins was demonstrated in the ensuing months as business climbed to higher and higher levels.

The House of McKesson & Robbins, which Coster had rebuilt—and looted—during the Depression, flourished beautifully after his death. Relieved of the drain of the fictitious Canadian subsidiary, it rode apace into the lush prewar economy of 1939-40. In 1940, before interest payments and federal taxes, the company netted almost $6,000,000, higher than Coster's record year of 1937, when the balance sheet was inflated by the imaginary profits of the nonexistent crude-drug business.

Coster's suicide triggered one of the most involved and expensive investigations in criminal history. Hundreds of police officers, government agents, accountants, and attorneys spent millions of dollars trying to find the missing pieces of the McKesson & Robbins puzzle. Coster had juggled more than $135,000,000 in McKesson & Robbins money through more than 150 known banking and brokerage accounts. It was believed that the man of many aliases had many more accounts in banks and brokerage houses, but they were never discovered. Auditing teams were able to identify only $3,200,000 as stolen money. The cost of trying to determine the extent of Coster's defalcations was far greater than the amount earmarked by the auditors' inconclusive report.

A typical example of Coster's devious methods was the game of musical chairs he played with the Anglo-French Finance Corporation only a few months before his debacle. The post-mortem investigation disclosed that this company was incorporated under letters patent of the Dominion of Canada on August 20, 1938, with a capital stock of 1,000 shares without par value. Even with Thompson breathing down his neck, Coster did not hesitate to wheel and deal. And he showed a fiction-writer's flair for concocting firm names.

The Anglo-French Finance Corporation was wholly owned by the Anglo-Swiss Acceptance Corporation, Ltd. The latter company was wholly owned by the Fairfield Corporation, Ltd., a corporation registered in the Bahamas. The Fairfield

Corporation, Ltd., brings us home again, for it was owned 50 percent by P. Horace Girard (risen from the dead to become again an alias for F. Donald Coster), and 50 percent by John J. Jenkins, one of Mrs. Coster's brothers.

On August 26, 1938, less than a week after incorporation, the Anglo-Swiss Acceptance Corporation, Ltd., bought all of the capital stock of Anglo-French Finance Corporation for $5,000. From this point onward, the complications are dizzying, but in its simplest form, this is what happened: Anglo-Swiss loaned Anglo-French $240,000, with which the latter purchased certain investments from the Acme Trading Corporation, a Massachusetts company. Using these investments as collateral, Anglo-French borrowed $250,000 from McKesson & Robbins, Inc., on October 14, exactly two months before Coster's arrest. Two weeks later, on November 2, Anglo-French borrowed another $25,000 from McKesson & Robbins, Inc. On November 15, Anglo-French loaned $25,000 to McKesson & Robbins. All this curious legerdemain was probably a preliminary step in some new scheme to drain funds from the McKesson & Robbins treasury.

When the trustee caught up with this adroit feat of fiscal juggling, Anglo-Swiss had $54,789.23 on deposit with the Royal Bank of Canada. Anglo-French had $29,565.63 in an account at the same bank. What happened to the other $165,645.14 of proceeds from the McKesson & Robbins loan no one has ever been able to find out. The stock certificates of Fairfield Corporation, Ltd., and the Anglo-Swiss Acceptance Corporation had been sent to the home of F. Donald Coster in Fairfield, pursuant to his instructions, but neither the trustee nor the federal and state investigators were able to locate the certificates. Wardall, as trustee, finally recovered the balance of the two firms' bank accounts for McKesson & Robbins.

After miles of headlines and many months of sound and fury, the long-drawn-out investigations and hearings by the probers and prosecutors proved to be anticlimactic. Leaks to the press in the early stages of the inquiry strongly intimated that some of the most important figures in banking and investment circles in both New York and Connecticut would be indicted. Scareheads screamed that the discovery of Coster's "diaries" and a "little brown book" promised sensational developments.

A postal inspector discovered these documents in the shack in which George Dietrich had hidden them, and immediately turned them over to his superiors. U.S. District Attorney Lamar Hardy deemed the find so important that he boarded an early train for Washington, accompanied by his aides Gregory Noonan and Irving R. Kaufman, to deliver the "astounding evidence" to Assistant Attorney General Brien McMahon personally. According to federal officials, the books contained "personal records, business records, copies of correspondence, and every conceivable detail of his [Coster's] life and activities between the years 1920 and his death. Only the years between 1928 and 1930 are missing. The books contain in detail the names, records, and sums involved in Coster's enterprises, both legitimate and illicit, and the names of his blackmailers and the amounts paid them."

This was a startling development whetting the public's appetite for new sensational disclosures. Headlines blared anew across the country. The New York *Daily News* shrilled EIGHT BLACKMAILERS ROBBED COSTER. The *Herald Tribune* added TWO KNOWN RACKETEERS FACE ARREST FOR COLLECTIONS

FROM DRUG SWINDLER. The New York *Times* sedately stated
BLACKMAIL CLUES FOUND. Investigating officers operating under the perennial guise of "informed sources" indicated there
was reason to believe that Coster's payments to blackmailers
could go as high as $5,000,000 bled out of his plunder during
the decade before his death. The obvious excitement of the
federal attorneys in their precipitate rush to Washington with
the "little brown book and diaries" lent credence to the reports that the blackmailers were about to be exposed. Investigators also intimated that Benjamin Simon, the Coster payoff
man, had pointed the finger at some of the biggest names in
the underworld, listing them as regular members of the shakedown club. They had paid Coster fortunes for his high-alcohol-
content products during their Prohibition era harvest and
had been getting their money back in lavish payments for
their silence. Coster had been unable to escape from the
ghosts of his checkered past, in the Adelphi and Girard companies as well as McKesson & Robbins. Rumors brought up
the names of practically every top man in the crime world
from Johnny Torrio and Al Capone to Dutch Schultz and
Legs Diamond.

An even more exciting facet of the promised disclosures,
particularly for the home-town folks, was the intimation that
important politicians, police officers, and other influence ped-
dlers were also "fingered" by Simon and the explosive "little
brown book." Somewhere, somehow, during the trip to Washington the "little brown book" lost its dynamite. Officialdom,
originally so excited about its revelations, became either
tongue-tied or completely mute at any mention of its her-
alded potency. Then as other phases of the case took over the
headlines, the interest in Coster's personal records waned and
finally died. These relatively slim diaries were overshadowed

by the nearly two tons of documents introduced into evidence when the indictments were finally brought into court a year and a half after Coster's death. But despite the time consumed by the investigations and the awesome volume of the exhibits, the list of defendants was sadly unimpressive.

Only nine men were indicted for complicity in Coster's fraudulent operations. Six of the nine were obviously puppets of the swindler—his three brothers, two brothers-in-law, and Benjamin Simon. Of the imposing gallery of top men in the financial world associated with the building of the McKesson & Robbins empire, only three relatively minor directors of the Connecticut group were indicted: Horace Merwin, Bridgeport banker; Rowley W. Phillips, Waterbury investment banker; and John H. McGloon, the company comptroller. As the cases against these men were presented, it became apparent that the prosecution was depending more upon sheer tonnage of evidence than damaging proof that the men were any more than victims of a criminal genius. The government's case contained more holes than a wheel of Emmentaler cheese.

True, the prosecution was handicapped by the absence of one key witness: Julian Thompson, the one man who might have cleared up some of the mysteries muddying Coster's financial manipulations. Thompson had started digging into the smelly muck before George Dietrich had tried to sweeten the atmosphere by stripping the files and vault of damaging information when the receivership action was begun in Hartford. Federal, state, and Stock Exchange representatives kept up a tremendous pressure on Thompson as they competed for his presence at their hearings. It was all too much for the sensitive, high-principled Princetonian.

Thompson shrank from the spotlight that picked him out

as a stellar performer in the three-ring circus the press had made of the Coster-Musica case. Everything about it was distasteful. He was horrified by the fact that the probers and prosecutors seemed more interested in creating sensational headlines than in seeking the truth. He cringed at the realization that he had actually introduced and then for years supported an impostor. He could not sleep at night for the knowledge that he was identified as Coster's original sponsor and his ultimate nemesis. The emotional strain of testifying, day after day, left him so shaken, so disgusted with the lurid publicity, that he wept when he got home at night. He lost weight.

Four months after Coster's suicide, Thompson caught cold. His weakened constitution could not withstand the infection. The cold developed into influenza. Pneumonia threatened. He seemed to have lost the will to live. On April 21, 1939, two days before his fifty-first birthday, Julian Thompson died in his New York apartment at 823 Park Avenue. He had been ill only a week.

If there had ever been any doubt that he was not one who had grown rich with the growth of McKesson & Robbins, the records of the Fairfield County probate court settled it once and for all. His estate at his death was valued at $41,000.

Another man who might have been a key witness was William T. Truxtun, an old associate of Coster's dating back to the Mount Vernon days. Truxtun had been general Prohibition administrator for New York state when Coster organized Girard & Co. and drew thousands of gallons of alcohol monthly from government warehouses to be converted into hair tonic and other products that could readily be reconverted to "imported Scotch whisky." That early relationship between Coster and Truxtun must have been highly satisfactory, for after Coster became president of McKesson & Robbins, he still did business with Truxtun. In fact, after Repeal threw Truxtun out of work, Coster sent him to Canada to establish a mail-drop address for McKesson & Robbins, Ltd., the fictional crude-drug division.

Federal prosecutors wanted very much to question Truxtun, but could find no trace of him. A nation-wide search ended where it had begun—in Connecticut. The trail ended in Waterbury, where Truxtun had lived for several years. He was not to testify. His body had been found in a swamp in the town of Middlebury, a few miles outside of Waterbury, in 1935. The coroner's verdict, "accidental drowning," was subjected to a searching newspaper review, particularly as there had been no autopsy.

As there was no logical explanation of Truxtun's presence in the area where he was found lying in a shallow stream, hardly deep enough to drown a man in command of his faculties, foul play was suspected. Investigators soon ran into a blank wall, however, when they found that the coroner who had reported "accidental death" without a post-mortem examination could not be questioned. He, too, was dead when Coster's "accomplices" came to trial.

As witness followed witness in the McKesson & Robbins case being tried in federal court in New York City, it became apparent that the principal target of the prosecution was Horace B. Merwin, the handsome, popular Bridgeport civic leader who had succeeded Clinton Barnum Seeley as president of the Bridgeport-City Trust Company. Rowley W. Phillips, general manager of R. F. Griggs & Co. of Waterbury, another of the early backers of Coster, was a more militant defendant. After finding Phillips a tartar on the stand, government lawyers directed most of their questions at the more reserved Merwin. Phillips, Merwin, and McGloon, the comptroller, all pleaded not guilty.

In a public statement issued after his indictment, Merwin set the tone for the defense. He said:

> I have been entirely innocent of any knowledge of the guilty acts of the late F. Donald Coster. . . . Like thousands of others including the many employees of the company, I at all times had implicit faith in the officers as well as the annual report of its auditors, a firm of internationally-known certified public accountants. . . .
>
> As far as my connection with the firm is concerned, I had no reason to feel anything but pride in it, and gratification at the payrolls and the money that had been brought into the community, until the shocking disclosure as to Mr. Coster's true identity and the falsity of the statements which had been accepted in good faith by the accountants. . . . I have no fear that the utmost probe of the facts will show that at any time I did anything for which I need apologize or feel ashamed.

The trial of the three Connecticut "accomplices" opened in New York City before federal Judge Grover M. Moscowitz on March 7, 1940, almost fifteen months after Coster's suicide. The prosecution had collected a mountain of evidence and interviewed more than a thousand witnesses. George and Robert Dietrich, George Vernard, and Benjamin Simon had pleaded guilty a year before and were prepared to take the stand as witnesses for the government. The defendants were represented by a battery of eminent barristers headed by George Z. Medalie for Merwin, Harold Corbin for Phillips, and Frederick Ironsides for McGloon.

Battle lines were sharply drawn and the strategy of the trial was quickly revealed in the opening address of opposing counsel. Although the lawyers for the defense were so numerous that they could not all be seated at the same large table, it was clear from the outset that Medalie, a former U.S. district attorney and a distinguished trial lawyer, would be their spokesman. His opening remarks took more than three hours. His colleagues spoke only briefly. Pitted against Medalie was U.S. Attorney Irving R. Kaufman, a brilliant young prosecutor, and a staff of seven.

From the start it was evident that the underlying interest in the case was not the guilt or innocence of the three defendants, or even the manner or magnitude of their alleged crime. The phantom defendant on trial was F. Donald Coster, and the issue was whether or not his masquerade had been artful enough to have deceived honest men.

Medalie in his opening painted Coster as a genius.

"Coster's impersonation was the greatest and most brilliant deception in the history of the world," he said. He went on to assert that Coster's phenomenal success in fooling the most astute leaders of the world in finance and business made it easy to understand his success in deceiving "small city bankers."

Not so, insisted Kaufman, who called the defendants knowing accomplices, and downgraded Coster as a "small-timer of unsavory reputation who could not have got to first base in this huge swindle without the aid of these men."

"Coster, the great executive, the Horatio Alger of our story, committed suicide," Kaufman went on. "Investigations . . . revealed that this was not a one-man show at all. Coster had help, plenty of help. They needed one another. They all needed Coster and Coster needed them."

Throughout the trial, Medalie tried to create the portrait of a business wizard while Kaufman strove to prove that Coster was more the tool of the financiers than master of the McKesson & Robbins empire.

Prime witness for the prosecution was George Dietrich, who proved an excellent government witness in response to Kaufman's direct examination. His testimony had the ring of authority and sincerity, as he described meetings and conversations indicating that the defendants had been aware of Coster's modus operandi. As he testified, Medalie was quick to spot his Achilles' heel to be exploited on cross-examination. Each time Kaufman tried to downgrade Coster, Dietrich balked. It was soon apparent that the witness held his dead brother in such high esteem that, although he was willing to entrap the bankers, he would not do so at the expense of Coster's reputation. There was a noticeable trace of pride in his voice every time he spoke of "Mr. Coster."

On cross-examination Medalie dangled this fraternal pride before the witness and Dietrich rose to the bait. "I always thought my brother was a smart and honest man," he said. "He had a bug to do things in a big way." The defense attorney led him into increasingly boastful statements about his brother's brilliance until he finally declared that the firm's problems had arisen chiefly because the other members of the company hierarchy were not intelligent enough to keep pace with Coster.

Medalie also elicited testimony that in its final year of Coster's stewardship, McKesson & Robbins made $150,000,000 worth of real sales of pharmaceuticals, biologicals, and popular remedies, as compared to "only $19,000,000 in paper sales of crude drugs."

In cross-examining Nathan Frankel, an F.B.I. accountant appearing for the prosecution, Medalie drew the admission that Coster's administration of the company had weathered both the Depression and his frauds with a good margin to spare. Frankel agreed that the real business organized by Coster was so much larger than its fictitious business when he shot himself in December of 1938 that the huge drug house was actually "solvent." He testified that he had worked steadily on the company's books for three months and had found that, after casting out all imaginary transactions, the real earnings of McKesson & Robbins under Coster's direction were always enough to pay interest on its outstanding debentures of $16,000,000, plus dividends on 500,000 shares of preferred stock, and, in his final year, enough to pay a twenty-five-cent dividend on each of more than 1,250,000 shares of common stock.

Medalie asked Frankel: "Can we safely say that after the elimination of the fictitious profits the real net profit was not less than $2,100,000 in 1937? And that after paying interest on the outstanding debentures and dividends on preferred stock, there was still $300,000 available for dividends on common stock, if declared?"

"I would say so," Frankel answered.

Throughout the trial it was made evident that while Merwin and his fellow defendants might have misjudged Coster's moral values, they were much more sagacious in assaying his worth as a business executive. Taking the stand in his own defense, Merwin testified that the $6,000 he had originally invested in 1925 and 1926 within three years grew into a quarter of a million dollars through various mergers.

"We had been with Coster from the start," Merwin testified. "We never noticed that Coster's [Canadian] activities never brought in any actual cash. Since recent developments I have wondered why we weren't suspicious, and accepted reports of increased inventories and accounts receivable in the crude-drug department. But we . . . had the utmost faith in Mr. Coster. He was a most unusual man and had shown remarkable progress in the management of the company over a long period of years."

Rowley Phillips, the Waterbury investment banker, was queried about his position during the power struggle between Waddill Catchings and Coster when Catchings suggested deposing the president. Said Phillips: "I believed then and I believe now that Coster knew the drug business inside out. I do not believe Catchings knew it. Coster was the horse on which we bet. Catchings didn't say anything about the crude-drug department."

To support his statement, Phillips produced a copy of Catchings' report to the directors.

Summing up for the defense, Medalie, Corbin, and Ironsides joined forces to try to convince the jury that Coster's impersonation was such a masterpiece that they themselves would have believed him. Their eloquent pleas were spiced by such words as "wizard . . . fabulous . . . genius . . . amazing . . . hypnotic." They spoke glowingly of his "tremendous success in legitimate business" as proof of his ability to have been the "sole perpetrator of the fraud."

Kaufman's closing argument for the prosecution spared no effort to belittle the dead man's talents and to place full responsibility for the conspiracy on his financial backers.

When the trial finally ended after ten weeks (to the day) of emotion-packed oratory, the question remained the same as it was when it was first expressed in the opening statements of opposing counsel. The jury had to decide whether Coster had been a combination of Horatio Alger, Robin Hood, and Ivar Kreuger, as asserted by the defense, or a petty, incompetent thief aided and abetted by greedy bankers, as claimed by the prosecution.

In a two-hour charge to the jury, Judge Moscowitz restated the question. He declared that the three defendants were "either victims or parties . . . in what lawyers call one of the greatest crimes of the century. Coster could not have committed the crime alone. Others have played a part. . . . If they are victims, they are not guilty. If they have played a guilty part, they are not innocent. Of course, I have an opinion as to the guilt and innocence of these defendants which I don't intend to express. The administration of law and justice is in your hands."

After a two-day session and thirteen hours of deliberation, the jurors informed the court that they had reached a verdict on two of the defendants. As they filed into the tensely silent courtroom and took their places in the jury box, the defendants watched with anxious eyes. The formalities were brief but agonizing. The clerk of the court called the roll of the jurors, then asked:

"Ladies and gentlemen of the jury, have you reached a verdict?"

"We have," replied Foreman James P. O'Neill.

"What is your verdict?"

"As to Rowley W. Phillips and Horace B. Merwin, not guilty on all counts."

"And so say you all?"

A murmur of "ayes" arose.

Amid the sudden jubilation that surrounded the two happy men, there was a poignant pocket of silence around the chair of John McGloon. There evidently had been many hours of wrangling over the case against the comptroller.

One juror later said that they had taken literally scores of ballots on McGloon.

When the jurors retired again to continue their deliberations on McGloon, they had run out of fight. They had been deadlocked over the comptroller for most of their thirteen hours, and with the Merwin and Phillips cases closed, the pro-McGloon holdouts were ready to compromise. The panel was back with its final verdict in forty-five minutes.

McGloon was found guilty on only one of the thirteen counts of the indictment—violation of the Securities and Exchange Act. He was found innocent on nine mail-fraud counts, two other Securities and Exchange Act counts, and a conspiracy charge. Some of the jurors had found it impossible to absolve all three of the defendants, and tapped McGloon for the most minor of the counts, more because of what he had not done than for what he had done. The jurors who held out for a guilty verdict believed he should have realized what was happening, faced up to Coster, and reported him to the S.E.C.

McGloon was sentenced to a year and a day prison term, and fined $5,000. The "accomplices" who had pleaded guilty a year earlier drew the following sentences: Benjamin Simon, three years; George Vernard, three years; George Dietrich, two and a half years; Robert Dietrich, one and a half years. John and Leonard Jenkins were each sentenced to a year and a day, but Leonard's sentence was suspended.

These feeble results of the long, expensive investigations and the long and lurid trials proved only that Coster had been the sole creative—though evil—genius behind the McKesson & Robbins story. His brothers, brothers-in-law, and Simon were merely his puppets who moved only when he pulled the strings, as he had explained in his suicide note.

McGloon, a subordinate beholden to Coster for his job, was hardly strong enough to challenge the dictatorial president of his firm, when even the wealthiest and most powerful of the directors deferred to him.

As for Merwin and Phillips, they were unwittingly dealing with a character completely alien to their milieu. They were early sponsors who had a tiger by the tail and couldn't or wouldn't let go while the company was producing such fabulous profits. It is significant that they held on to the bulk of their stockholdings throughout the crisis. They were basically bankers who knew little about the administrative details of a large corporation involved chiefly in manufacturing and distribution. Their primary interests were profit and growth. The government had apparently singled them out as symbols, for their connections with the firm were little different from those of many other financial backers who had furnished Coster with the golden rungs for his ladder to success.

20 : Restitution,
Rehabilitation, and
Blackmail

While the political prosecutors were fighting each other for newspaper headlines, William Wardall, the trustee, was quietly putting pressure on everyone who had profited from Coster's inflated balance sheets. He collected well over $500,000 from directors who, as stockholders, had shared generously in unwarranted dividend payments. Price, Waterhouse, although protesting they had performed all of the services for which they had been retained, returned more than $550,000 of the million-plus they had collected in fees over the years. The court to which Wardall was responsible approved this settlement, as well as the $135,000 Wardall collected on an insurance policy against fraud by employees or officers of the company. Wardall also collected $2,000,000 from other sources.

Although Wardall recovered well over $4,000,000 in his campaign for restitution, the sum was a picayune contribution to the company's solvency. Most of it went to defray the expenses of tracing Coster's fiscal acrobatics, the cost of reorganization, legal charges, and Wardall's own trusteeship fee. The biggest item was the expense of searching out the illicit operations, reauditing the books, and setting up an accountancy system for reorganization. For this job Wardall retained the outside auditing firm of S. D. Liedesdorf & Company, which, by October 9, 1941, had run up a bill of some $687,000. Many lawyers were involved in the reorganization problems, but the general attorneys for the trustee were Winthrop, Stimson, Putnam & Roberts, whose fees ran above $450,000. Wardall's own fee was $250,000.

Charges filed by Wardall on September 22, 1941, with the clerk of the United States District Court for the Southern District of New York added up to more than $2,275,000. Most of these charges were for services rendered the trustee. There were also fees of committees and counsel for various stockholders' and creditors' groups that totaled more than $700,000.

Wardall's major effort went into restoring confidence in McKesson & Robbins among the wholesalers, manufacturers, retailers, and the public. He retained the public relations firm of Baldwin, Beach & Mermey. He dispatched attorneys to the Food and Drug Administration in Washington to get a letter refuting charges that McKesson & Robbins had been a major offender in the distribution of misbranded drugs. Radio programs were sponsored and an unceasing barrage of news releases bombarded all media, particularly the trade press. In a regular series of forthright statements, Wardall presented the McKesson & Robbins case to the public. Monthly sales figures were paraded with all the fanfare and optimistic trappings his professional publicists could dig up or dream up.

Since "inventories" had become a key word in the crude-drug division scandal, Wardall ordered an exhaustive check of all merchandise on hand. This service alone cost the company $105,000, as well as many thousands of man-days by McKesson & Robbins employees. Every one of nearly 50,000 items in seventy-six company warehouses was checked for quality and quantity. The liquor stocks, even those stored in bonded warehouses, were analyzed. The complete line of 238 drugs manufactured by McKesson & Robbins was turned over to outside chemists for an objective report.

A large-scale campaign of newspaper advertising was launched in seventy carefully selected cities. The layouts were headed "Facts About McKesson & Robbins" and emphasized the fact that the firm had been in business for 106 years, that it employed 7500 people, and that its customers, from public to manufacturers, continued to express confidence in the company by purchasing its products.

As part of his campaign to rehabilitate the corporate image of McKesson & Robbins, Wardall sent two eloquent extroverts—W. E. Dewell, general manager, and Dr. A. L. Omohundro, director of laboratories—on a nation-wide tour. They addressed wholesalers, retailers, and any organization that would give them a platform and an audience. Sound pictures, brochures, placards, and every other conceivable visual aid were used in support of the carefully planned grand design. Employees were trained as good-will ambassadors. Dealers were brought to Fairfield from all over the country to sample the hospitality of the new management.

A major achievement in the drive to "Sell McKesson & Robbins to the Country" and make people forget the Coster scandal was a successful effort to induce the motion picture industry to abandon plans to film the strange story of Dr. Coster and Mr. Musica. Three topflight studios had already invested time and money in preparing a movie that would at that time have distorted the new image Wardall was trying so hard to project.

The solution to the mystery that is the unwritten last chapter of Coster's biography will probably never be found. What happened to the millions of dollars he bled from his enterprises?

Coster had woven a financial web of such intricate pattern that estimates of his pilferage varied by as much as $18,000,-000. That he could have kept track of the extremely active (though imaginary) traffic in crude drugs over the years seems almost incredible, yet he channeled the sales and purchases with the resultant ebb and flow of money through the company books so astutely that the fictitious deals could not be separated from normal business. Official appraisal of the actual loss to the company, based on balances finally struck by outside accountants, became a bookkeeping item of something more than $3,000,000.

The validity of this figure is largely academic. There is little or no record of the innumerable cash disbursements that took place casually in the large vault in George Dietrich's offices. Certainly there has never been a clear explanation of the $18,000,000 in inventories and accounts receivable of Mc-Kesson & Robbins, Ltd., items which reflected a constant drain on the parent company's treasury, year after year. Practically the only sums directly attributable to Coster's fraud were the $150,000 in commissions, the $18,000 annual fee to

W. W. Smith & Co., and the $12,000 annual retainer to Man-
ning & Co.

Where, then, did the money go? Neither Coster, the Dietrichs, nor any other member of the Musica family lived on
a scale that would have dissipated millions. All the brothers
drew salaries and had other sources of income more than sufficient to have paid for their living costs, prior to the debacle,
without touching a cent of the loot. Still, Coster, judged by
the standards and estates of men in his income bracket, died
a pauper except for his quarter-million-dollar insurance policy. He had deeded the Fairfield home to his wife and given
her substantial stockholdings. Inasmuch as his legitimate income in a single year—1937, as an example—came to more
than $400,000, while the Smith and Manning payments that
year totaled another $180,000, these gifts to his wife were
rather modest. His legitimate income, incidentally, broke
down as follows: salary, $40,000; dividends, $250,000; profit
from his brokerage account, $150,000.

Blackmail has been mentioned as a possible major drain
on Coster's resources. Coster himself referred to it in his suicide note. The secret and never-published diary and "little
brown book" were supposed to contain detailed information
as to people, amounts, and dates of payments. Rumors were
rife. Nowhere in the course of the lengthy investigations,
however, was any evidence produced that any substantial
amounts went into these payoffs.

Agents who at first had exulted over the revelations in the
"little brown book" were privately bitter when they intimated that it contained the names of so many politically sa-
cred cows that the entire list had to be suppressed. They
further admitted "off the record" that the shakedown directory also included some of the biggest names in the under-

world, many of them contacts and customers of the Prohibition era, whose big money had established Girard & Co. and helped Coster to rescue McKesson & Robbins from the jaws of the Depression. They had not forgotten their old alcohol supplier and he remembered them well enough to decide it was better to pay them than to challenge them.

One of these worthies was Arthur (Dutch Schultz) Flegenheimer, big-time bootlegger and acknowledged baron of the needle-beer trade during the life of the Volstead Act. Schultz remembered Coster very well indeed. In early 1935, Schultz moved the capital of his numbers-racket empire to Bridgeport, only a few miles away from the McKesson & Robbins plant and the lovely Coster mansion on Mill Plain Road, Fairfield. He set up headquarters in the Stratfield Hotel with a battalion of bodyguards headed by Lulu Rosenkrantz and Abe Landau, a pair of thugs whose muscles and guns were worth $7,500 a month in wages to Schultz. The Dutchman was guarded around the clock with men stationed across the street from the hotel and the lobby every hour of the day and night.

Shortly after his arrival in Bridgeport, Schultz boasted that he had come there because he had "influential friends in the area, men who carried a lot of weight even in Washington." He was at the time being pressured by internal-revenue agents in connection with his past income tax returns. Schultz had two strong recreational interests. One was poker, which he would play with anyone. The second, a bit more unusual for a racketeer, was horseback-riding. This he was quite private about, and when he went off for a canter, in the direction of Fairfield, only a squad from his bodyguard was permitted to accompany him.

Despite his known infamy as a gangland overlord, Schultz

made some interesting contacts on his own during his stay in Bridgeport. Not long after his arrival, he became a regular in the Saturday afternoon poker game in which prominent lawyers, politicians and businessmen had been playing for years. Some of these men recall that Bob Dietrich and Ben Simon seemed to know Schultz well enough to visit him at the hotel. They also remember that Dutch had evinced considerable interest in their opinion of Coster's importance in the community.

Both Schultz and Abe Landau had been inmates of the Tombs during the time when Musica-Johnson was associated with that institution. Landau was there awaiting trial at the time of Musica's release in 1916. Schultz was an inmate later in 1919, when Musica, then Johnson, was an investigator in the state's attorney's office. Coincidentally, one of Landau's fellow prisoners was Giuseppe Brandino, the thug who became a partner in the bootleg-alcohol supply station known as the Adelphi Pharmaceutical Manufacturing Company, created by Musica under the name of Frank D. Costa. This would indicate that Schultz and Landau were among Adelphi's earliest customers, who presumably would continue as clients of Girard and McKesson & Robbins.

On October 23, 1935, only weeks after he left Bridgeport, Schultz was mowed down by underworld assassins in the Palace Chop House in Newark, New Jersey. Also killed in the same volley of slugs from a 12-gauge shotgun and a brace of .45-caliber revolvers were three of his henchmen, Lulu Rosenkrantz, Abe Landau, and Otto Berman.

Schultz lingered for twenty-two hours after being shot. During his last four hours, he emerged from a complete coma and babbled wildly in the delirium of a 106-degree fever. A police stenographer sat at his bedside during these hours and took down every intelligible word. After Schultz succumbed, local and federal police officers familiar with his activities and associates attempted to cull out all of the relevant information in his disconnected utterances. They were able to identify almost all of the names mentioned and tie them into the rackets. However, it wasn't until more than three years later, in December of 1938, that two of the names seemed to make any sense—Phil and George. After the revelation that F. Donald Coster and George Dietrich were really Philip and George Musica, police recalled Schultz's stay in Bridgeport a short time before he was liquidated in Newark.

Phil and George had been the mystery names of Schultz's delirium. They had been uttered in the same sequence of sentences. First Schultz had muttered, "Now listen, Phil, fun is fun." His immediate next statement was, "George, don't make no fool moves." Dutch Schultz, fabled as a tight man with a penny, was hardly the type to let a sitting duck like Coster get away without paying for his silence. In a field where avarice was king, the Dutchman was recognized as the greediest of the lot. There were others who had known Coster as Musica-Johnson-Costa, who were undoubtedly members of the "little brown book" club.

While the law-enforcement agencies of two states and the federal government were frantically trying to get to the bottom of the McKesson & Robbins mystery, a score of suspected blackmailers were questioned and five were actually arrested. Three of these were subsequently released. Two were indicted.

The two brought to trial were Joseph and Mary Brandino, the strong-arm florists who had been Musica-Coster's partners in the Adelphi Pharmaceutical Manufacturing Company in Brooklyn. Their indictments covered seven counts of conspiracy, blackmail, and extortion, dating back to 1925, and involving payments—over some thirteen years—of $50,000.

The trial of the Brandinos revealed their weird attempts to stay within the law. They never actually demanded hush-money. They merely asked for loans—but they asked loud and clear. They besieged Coster with telegrams, telephone calls, and visits to Fairfield. They wanted only to "borrow" sums ranging from $100 to $3,000 to pay bills for everything under the sun—from medical care to mortgage interest. Their "begging letters," about as subtle and friendly as a poke in the ribs with the muzzle of a .45, were little "or else" notes from one alumnus of the Tombs to another, full of nostalgic reminiscences and deploring the fact that the public could not share their common memories. Coster always coughed up.

Some of the money to satisfy the Brandinos had come from Coster's own pocket—his income could absorb the bite pain-lessly—but much of the tribute exacted from him by a wide variety of people, not all of them blackmailers, came from the firm's coffers. This was particularly true of handouts to politicians and policemen. A revolving slush fund of $70,000 was established for this purpose. It was administered by George Dietrich and replenished at the rate of $2,000 a month, a relatively picayune sum identified on the company books as a cash item to defray costs of entertainment and lob-bying.

Where then did the millions go?

In his suicide note, Coster had written: ". . . and know there are no hidden treasures anywhere." And yet Coster early in his career had demonstrated a very great talent for hiding his assets. Edward Hubbard, Mrs. Coster's first hus-band, first met his successor when he was retained to search for money and property belonging to Philip Musica after the human-hair swindle. He failed utterly. Years later Coster twitted Hubbard about his inability to find the missing wealth and boasted about the cleverness of his concealment. In addition to the hundreds of thousands of dollars he chiseled from bankers in this country and abroad, there was also the little matter of the million dollars Mama Assunta Musica borrowed, on the basis of her Neapolitan barbershop sweepings, and somehow mislaid somewhere in Italy. And the hair-hoax windfalls came before the advent of the income tax and the Bureau of Internal Revenue investigators.

Despite his emphatic disclaimer, Coster's "hidden treasure" is still an exciting conversation piece among the older residents of Fairfield and the veteran employees of McKesson & Robbins. Many of these people, perhaps with tongue in cheek, would invest eagerly in a map purporting to pinpoint the location of Coster's buried wealth. Any map relating to an area within the cruising range of the *Carolita* would be snapped up. Townspeople still chuckle over the gold-rush fever that struck Fairfield when it was learned that there was no money in Coster's bank accounts or safe-deposit boxes. For several nights thereafter, the Coster grounds on Mill Plain Road resounded to the soft echoes of furtive digging.

One of those chuckling the longest was a Fairfield policeman who did a little treasure-hunting of his own. He had been acquainted with Coster for some time and remembered the many hours the McKesson & Robbins president used to spend with his dogs, particularly his favorite Saint Bernard. The more he thought about it, the more convinced he became that if Coster had buried his loot anywhere on the grounds, it would be under the Saint Bernard's doghouse that was set apart from the kennels housing the chows.

Loaded down with digging equipment and carrying several pounds of choice meat liberally doused with a sleeping potion, the policeman and two cronies crept into the Coster yard shortly after midnight. . . .

Next morning there was a new mystery to add to the long list of post-mortem puzzles left behind by F. Donald Coster. Why had the Saint Bernard's doghouse been moved a dozen feet from its usual site? Why, with the sun already high in the heavens, was the big dog, still chained to his doghouse, still fast asleep? Why had a deep pit been dug where the doghouse used to be?

It was several weeks before the policeman, who for years had made a fetish of avoiding manual labor, would admit the truth about his blistered hands. Breaking through the concrete flooring of the doghouse had been hard work. And there had been no buried treasure.

Wardall and his auditors had little more success than Hubbard or the amateur treasure hunters of Fairfield in locating the fortune Coster was believed to have amassed. Even the $3,000,000 officially set as the amount of Coster's embezzlement could not be located. His shares in the company, appraised at about a million dollars, could not be traced, despite exhaustive checking of the several dummy accounts he had used. Investigators did learn that during the weeks preceding his suicide, Coster was engaged in a dizzy whirl of buying and selling stocks through accounts held in his wife's name and in John Jenkins' name, as well as through his own account. Suspicion that he was also trading under several aliases could not be verified.

A large amount of cash known to be in George Dietrich's vault a few days before the receivership action was filed in Hartford was not there when Attorney Weisman, as receiver, came down to change locks and combinations. The money was evidently removed with the records by Dietrich at his brother's instigation.

An indication that Coster's estate would not be very large was first given in Fairfield twelve days after the suicide when Probate Court Judge Bradford Boardman set the surety bond for Mrs. Coster as executrix at only $10,000. This bond is usually based on twice the estimated debts plus the inheritance taxes. The judge obviously knew that there was not enough in the estate to meet these obligations. Judge Boardman appointed two lawyers, Adrian Maher and William E. Allen, Jr., as appraisers recommended by Samuel Reich, counsel for Mrs. Coster. He named Attorney Edward L. Kelly as the third appraiser.

Attachments and court orders had already impounded some $200,000 in stocks, bonds, and other securities, assets not included in the general inventory of the estate. Two and one-half years later, on March 10, 1942, Judge Boardman approved a petition for settlement of claims against these holdings. The Internal Revenue Bureau settled its claims for $77,000. Another $124,000 was turned over to McKesson & Robbins as satisfaction of the claim by Wardall as trustee that Coster had obtained the money by defrauding the company.

The largest single asset of Coster's personal estate was the yacht *Carolita,* appraised at $35,000. This was a tremendous markdown from its once assessed valuation of $250,000. The yacht was sold at public auction on June 10, 1939. Bidding was opened by a local man, John Corrigan of the Pequot Yacht Club, who offered $50. The *Carolita* was finally knocked down to Edward A. Cooper, a Chicago attorney, for

$15,000. Most of the proceeds of the sale went to pay out-standing bills against the yacht.

The final accounting of the Coster estate was handled by Probate Court Judge John P. Flanagan of the Bridgeport district, after Judge Ned O. Ostmark of Fairfield had disqual-ified himself as a trustee of the estate. Final figures showed that the original inventory of $55,000 had shrunk to a mere $505. Besides the yacht (its value absorbed by creditors), items listed were: wearing apparel, books, and personal effects, $200; twenty shares of stock in the Bridgeport University Club, $100; cash, $205. Charges against the estate included funeral costs of $1344. Taxes, administrators' and attorneys' fees, court costs and expenses ate up the rest of Coster's visible assets.

The home in Fairfield was in Carol Coster's name. She lived there alone for more than ten years after Coster's sui-cide. On July 10, 1949, she remarried there. Her third hus-band was Albert B. Carver of New York City. Five years later, Carol Jenkins Hubbard Carver sold the mansion and one acre of land for $65,000, and moved to Florida with her new husband. The purchaser, Carmen Tortora of Bridgeport, con-verted the place into a convalescent home which he named "The Carolton." Later Tortora bought the rest of the prop-erty.

The pet charity of the former chatelaine of The Carolton, the Fairfield Free Heart Clinic, was closed for lack of funds. And the Grand Lodge of the Free and Accepted Masons of Connecticut waived all claim to the cemetery Coster had fi-nanced in Bethel. The cemetery association asked permission of the court to surrender the property to McKesson & Rob-bins. The court approved the transfer.

*   *   *

Mama Assunta, so proud of having brought such a son into life, was not there to see him ushered out of it. At the first hint of the scandal, Dr. Petrovitz warned daughter Grace that the news might be fatal to the seventy-nine-year-old woman. Grace, who like her mother used the name Marie Girard, immediately spirited the ailing woman off to Miami in the seclusion of a train compartment. Mama Assunta was to outlive her infamous son by almost three years. She died at her Long Island home in October, 1941, at the age of eighty-one, and after a Roman Catholic service at St. Brigid's Church, was buried in the family plot in St. Rood's Cemetery at Westbury, Long Island.

Robert Dietrich was the only one of her sons to attend her funeral. The baby of the Musica boys was released from Lewisburg Federal Penitentiary in Pennsylvania in August, 1941. He moved his family from Connecticut to New Rochelle, New York, and had the courage to start over again from scratch. He went to work as traffic manager for the Suburban Leather Goods Company of Brooklyn. He died in New Rochelle on June 8, 1956, and was also buried in the family plot in Westbury.

George Dietrich was released from Lewisburg in May, 1942. He too had the courage to make a fresh start, and in the very community that saw his disgrace. He returned to Fairfield and went to work for the Grasmere Development Company for the remaining five years of his life. He died at Roslyn Park Hospital on Long Island on November 27, 1947. He too was buried with the Musicas in St. Rood's Cemetery in Westbury.

George Vernard was released from Lewisburg in September, 1942, and immediately disappeared from public view. The surviving Musica sisters disappeared not long after the suicide of the fair-haired boy from Mulberry Bend, who died rather than acknowledge his past.

Even in death Philip does not rest with the other Musicas in the family plot in St. Rood's Cemetery in Westbury. Aloof as always, he lies alone in his crypt in the Cyprus Hills mausoleum, F. Donald Coster for all eternity.

Three and one-half years after his appointment, William J. Wardall was released of his responsibility as trustee by federal Judge Coxe, who signed the final decree approving the reorganization plan for McKesson & Robbins. The firm had been returned to private ownership the year before on July 1, 1941. Wardall's plan had also been approved by the Securities and Exchange Commission and various stockholders' groups. Investors demonstrated their confidence in McKesson & Robbins when they eagerly purchased new debentures and preferred stock offered to finance the reorganization program. The firm had proved itself. By triumphantly coming through the ordeal by fire brought on by Coster himself, it had made Coster's dream of success come true.

A quarter of a century after Coster's final annual report for 1937, the Standard and Poor report of July 2, 1962, circulated by leading brokers, read in part:

> McKesson & Robbins has no counterpart in American business, since it is the only company that wholesales drugs, alcoholic beverages, and chemicals on a national scale. Although the declining prices of drugs have had an adverse effect on earnings, long-term prospects are favored by the recent move into generic drugs, the continued development of new pharmaceuticals, and rising demand for chemicals in less than carload lots. The issue is regarded as a worthwhile holding.

The report showed that the company had net sales of nearly $708,000,000 in 1961. It also stated that dividends had been paid "continuously since resumption in 1942," that the company had 9,000 employees and 22,000 shareholders. In summary, the picture of McKesson & Robbins is not only bright and shining today, but it is painted in the colors chosen by F. Donald Coster.

The Standard and Poor reference to generic drugs, reinforced a year later by stories in the New York *Herald Tribune,* must have brought poignant memories to the minds of Coster's associates in the 1920's when his interest in crude drugs was an aggressive (and successful) attempt to break monopolies rather than a fraudulent system of mail drops in Canada. The *Herald Tribune* on September 12, 1963, reported the McKesson & Robbins efforts to introduce low-priced generic drugs into Latin-America in competition with the much more expensive brand names, and that the 140-member Pharmaceutical Manufacturers Association had been fighting the move. Generic drugs bear chemical names known to doctors all over the world and require none of the expensive promotion that raises the price of brand names for the same compounds. Said the *Herald Tribune:*

> The struggle began when Colombia published a new decree last year proclaiming a new generic drug program and invited all major drug firms to participate. The only American firm to join the experiment was McKesson. . . .
> McKesson marketed thirty-two pain-killing life-saving drugs at dramatically low prices. An antibiotic used in treatment of respiratory infections and typhoid sold for 3.6 cents per capsule, compared with the trade-name product that sold for 29 cents. An arthritic was able to buy a month's supply of prednisilone for $2 instead of the $16 it had cost before. . . . The

drug industry in Colombia, which includes fifteen American firms, fought back. . . .

The old-timers must have heard nostalgic echoes of Coster's attack on the iodine trust in Chile, the bismuth monopoly in Bolivia, and the closed quinine market in Indonesia and Holland.

But Coster's ghost raised cautious echoes, too. At the bottom of the favorable 1962 report on McKesson & Robbins by Standard and Poor, there is a haunting little line in small, frightened type. It reads:

Information has been obtained from sources believed to be reliable, but its accuracy and completeness, and that of the opinions based thereon, are not guaranteed.

21 : The Anatomy of Skulduggery

DISTINGUISHED Americans who have been dead for twenty-five years are eligible for election to the Hall of Fame on the campus of New York University. Were there a World Hall of Infamy, there is little doubt that F. Donald Coster's bust would occupy a prominent niche in the Gallery of Corporate Finaglers. The list of outstanding nominees would not be a long one. It would certainly include the names of such fabled predators as Ivar Kreuger, Samuel Insull, Serge Alexandre Stavitsky, and Charles Ponzi. Even in this imposing company, Coster is unique. By the brazen brilliance and dizzy pace of his adventure, he rates as the most remarkable rogue of all.

F. Donald Coster, M.D., Ph.D., a completely fictional character, was thirty-nine years old in 1923 when he was created by Philip Musica out of whole cloth woven with threads gleaned along the route from the slums of Mulberry Bend through a cell block in the Tombs to Girard & Co. in Mount Vernon. Just three years later, in 1926, the purely imaginary

Dr. Coster calmly signed a check for a million dollars and assumed the presidency of McKesson & Robbins, one of the oldest and most highly respected drug firms in the country. His associates, all men of impeccable status in social, business, and financial circles, were awed by his genius and subservient to his will. Though his diplomas from Heidelberg were non-existent, there was no doubt about the authenticity of his Freemason's apron, his Shriner's fez, or his memberships in the New England Genealogical Society and the most exclusive clubs of New York and suburban Connecticut. As a widely known yachtsman, clubman, and master of an $87,-000,000 corporation, Dr. F. Donald Coster was in every sense the peer of his fellow biographees in *Who's Who in America*. Dr. Coster was also a swindler, a forger, and an impostor. Above all, he was a consummate actor. Once "Dr. Coster" appeared on stage, Philip Musica never for a moment emerged from the wings.

On the morning after his suicide, the New York *Times* editorially applauded his masterpiece in masquerade. Said the *Times:*

> Philip Musica achieved what in the field of pure art would have to be called a magnificent act of creation. . . . He was Frank Donald Coster, one might say, as Maurice Evans is Hamlet, as Joe Jefferson was Rip Van Winkle.

All of the others—Kreuger, Insull, Stavitsky, *et al*—faced the occupational hazards of fraud, but only Coster wore the insolent mask and nerve-rasping cloak of the impostor. Around every corner a pointing finger, like a witch's wand, waited to turn the moment into midnight when his yacht would become a clamshell and his home a hovel in the slums. His counterparts in crime had nothing to conceal but their current chicaneries. Their families and their fingerprints were free of menace. Coster was devoted to his family, but he could not acknowledge them openly without exposing his past. He alone of all the Musicas was artful enough to wear the Coster domino. His real name like his fingerprints carried the menace of swift truth—handicaps unknown to the rest of his confreres in adventure.

Publication of his true identity was a lethal blow to the president of McKesson & Robbins. F. Donald Coster was dead from the moment that his fingerprints matched those of Philip Musica. He could never live with, or as, the boy from Mulberry Bend. It was impossible for him to walk among those who had looked up to him and feel them looking down. The bullet he sent into his brain was only a punctuation mark in his obituary. This was tersely summed up by Dr. Henry Garrett, professor of psychology at Columbia University. Said Dr. Garrett: "Psychologically, Musica had wiped out his past when he became Coster. It would have been impossible for him to go back."

Coster is still a legendary figure, and people still speculate on what great feats he might have achieved if only he had been able to rid himself of his compulsive dishonesty. Some of those who knew him recall him only as a cruel fraud and a conscienceless thief. Others have memories of a shy philanthropist, a combination of Robin Hood and a Horatio Alger hero. His stunned colleagues, while declaring they had been duped, placed greater emphasis on his genius than on their gullibility.

The Wall Street seismograph never fluctuated more wildly than it did under the successive shocks of the last eleven days of Coster's life. McKesson & Robbins' thirty-five-state empire rocked under the impact of the surprise equity receivership, the revelation of a multimillion-dollar fraud, exposure of the

Musica masquerade, and finally the shattering news of Coster's suicide. Since he had played the role of F. Donald Coster for only fifteen years, few people could truthfully claim to know him well. His closest associates had been acquainted with him for little more than a decade. On one opinion, however, there was unanimity. It was generally agreed that the explosive growth of McKesson & Robbins in such an incredibly brief period was due to his wizardry.

Perhaps the most amazing factor in Coster's stewardship of the giant drug firm was that he built the greatest measure of its strength during the economy-wrecking Depression of the early '30's. Even the great Ivar Kreuger was sucked under by the ebb tide of liquid cash. The Match King had worked his miracles in the mad flood tide of the '20's when everything was moving upward. When the tide turned, he floundered about, desperately trying to recoup. Frustration and despair put a gun in his hand and a bullet through his heart in a luxurious Paris apartment on March 12, 1932. Coster fought his way through the terrible days of the early '30's, only to stumble at the threshold of the business boom of pre-World War II. The door to prosperity was already ajar when he met his bullet in the closing days of 1938.

Perhaps the most tragic victim of Coster's guile was Julian Thompson, the soft-spoken, erudite company treasurer. Thompson had such a tremendous regard for Coster's abilities that he became unwittingly the most cooperative pawn in his superior's chess game. When he realized how cruelly he had been deceived, he became Coster's nemesis. Although his suspicions and relentless probing actually triggered Coster's downfall, he got small satisfaction out of exposing the mountebank he had helped create. There is little doubt that his disillusionment hastened his death a few months after Coster's suicide. Yet despite his bitter disappointment in the man he trusted, Thompson recalled: "Everyone was in awe of his brilliance. All deferred to him in matters of importance."

Coster was a mysterious, controversial, dualistic man. The wake of his life trailed through the chambers of inquiry and the courts in the eloquent clash of eulogy with vituperation, tribute against scorn. His adherents praised him with wild extravagance. His detractors reviled him with bitter semantics. There was no middle ground. Everything was black or white, evil or virtuous. There were no grays. Yet somehow, sometimes there emerged a checkered pattern of the two at once, a mixture of black and white without blend, without compromise.

Attorney George Z. Medalie put it this way:

> Coster was a man of phenomenal ability. His methods were so diabolically clever that no one for a moment would have suspected them. Coster's impersonation was the greatest, the most brilliant in the history of the world, as brilliant as his own legitimate success.

This sophistic portrait was drawn on behalf of Medalie's client Merwin during his trial for alleged complicity. There was no such paradox in the statement made by Wilbur L. Cummings, a company director, at an attorney general's hearing. Cummings said:

> We knew of him as a skilled man, considering him a man of considerable substance and wealth. We all have the most implicit confidence in Mr. Coster. He is the father of the company and his whole executive force is with him.

The most scathing criticism of Coster was delivered by New York Supreme Court Justice Ferdinand Pecora, who described him as "the most diabolical, ingenious, sly man I have ever come in contact with. It was only when you looked into his eyes that you discovered a furtive look that aroused suspicion in you. I recall definitely that my suspicions of the man were aroused immediately the first time I looked into his eyes."

In contrast with Pecora's scornful words was the glowing panegyric of Alfred L. Becker, with whom Coster, as William Johnson, had once worked. Speaking before a Senate committee in 1919, Becker said of Coster:

> I have had the pleasure of watching the coming to life of a beautiful spirit, a beautiful Christian spirit in a man, which convinces me that there is such a thing as reform. There is no man in the world today whom I trust more. He is one of my best friends.

The most provocative question that floats in the mists of the Coster legend is what might have happened if Thompson had not forced the president's hand. Certainly no executive in the company felt or suspected any weakness in the firm's position when Coster exploded the surprise receivership. Coster's admirers point out that McKesson & Robbins survived both the multimillion-dollar fraud and the devastating scandal, and continued to grow and prosper without any significant change in the structure devised by the late president. George Dietrich expressed this point of view when he said:

> Had my brother been given more time, all of the money would have been put back. The inflation of the company's assets was necessary after the crash of 1929 in order to keep the company out of bankruptcy and afloat until the market recovered and they could sell more stock. Eventually my brother would have been able to put capital in place of the fictitious inventories and no one would have been hurt.

Dietrich was not alone in his belief that Coster somehow

might have extricated himself from the trap which he had set in the maze of Canadian mail drops but which Thompson had sprung. However, the problem of returning the $18,000,-000 represented by the audit figures of inventories and accounts receivable was a staggering one. Unless Coster had salted away a large part of this sum in some cache readily available only to him, it is difficult to see how he could have replaced it in a reasonable period of time. He would also have been faced with the problem of dissolving the Canadian subsidiary without causing undue alarm or suspicion. On the other hand, information developed during the inquiries indicates that Coster's imaginative maneuvers, amoral or immoral, did in fact carry the company through the Depression. The exhaustive check of his personal finances, although not completely informative, indicated that he used millions of his own dollars to bolster the stock in a collapsing market. There is other evidence, too, that he was driven more by vanity than by greed.

During his salad days, the first dollars from his ill-gotten gains went toward providing a luxurious home for his family and a lavish hotel suite for himself. He was an open-handed *bon vivant* running with the swiftest on Broadway. Later, the shaky economy of the Depression did not deter him from purchasing a seagoing yacht to go with his eighteen-room suburban mansion. His memberships in exclusive clubs were rarely used, but they were additional symbols of the long road he had traveled from Mulberry Bend. At the same time, those who were to status born were made to understand that while he was their peer, he was not one of them. He remained aloof, a person to be courted. F. Donald Coster granted local society leaders a small nod.

This was all heady champagne, but it was not the sudden

arrogance of a parvenu. Philip Musica had already been a snob in the vice-and-lice-ridden Little Italy of his youth. When he moved into his *pied-à-terre* in the Knickerbocker, consorted with Caruso and Scotti, was seen at the opera, and dined at Delmonico's and Bustanoby's, any change in his snobbishness was quantitative, not qualitative. His arrogance was only sharpened in the more selective environment of Connecticut's Fairfield County.

True, much of his aloofness and secrecy was part of his cover for his masquerade, but it was still an inherent factor of his personality. He maintained a life apart from his neighbors, his business associates, and his social peers because he considered them his inferiors. His colleagues, fellow directors, bankers, auditors, and lawyers, were to him parasites who grew fat and prosperous feeding on the corporate body he had created. Ego told him that this was his and his alone. His cynical amorality told him that it was right and just that he sluice off for his own use a generous share of the profits.

Many of his own statements support Dietrich's suggestion that Coster had a plan to avoid the cataclysm that was to end his career. It is not probable that the shallow fiction of the crude-drug trade could have been continued much longer without being exposed. His demonstrated ingenuity lends weight to the theory that he might have contrived a way out of his dilemma. He could have laid his problem before his colleagues and excused his deceit as the only alternative to bankruptcy during the Depression. Great actor that he was, he could certainly have spiced his confession with a stunning indictment of his associates for their complicity. They had participated in and profited from his fraud. They had approved his plans, taken stock bonuses, and shared dividends that they had voted on the basis of his inflated balance sheets. It would have been well within the domineering nature of F. Donald Coster to demand that they give him time to work out a plan for the restitution of missing funds and the reestablishment of an honest accounting system. Even honest, meticulous Julian Thompson, because of his great admiration for and confidence in Coster, might have granted him this respite.

Even had it been acceptable to Thompson, however, it is highly doubtful that Coster would have bought it. This is all conjecture, of course, but on the evidence available, Coster's plan must have been more devious and, to him, more logical. Coster could never have confessed to wrongdoing. The word did not exist in his vocabulary. For others, yes— there might be a difference between right and wrong. But in Coster's lexicon the great difference was between doing wrong and getting caught.

It was in Coster's nature to cheat. It was compulsive. He was repulsed by any plan or activity that held no personal advantage for him. He could not fit his great talents into the framework of society. His genius, if that is the word, could not be bridled. He must run into the wind, completely untrammeled. He must run headlong and blindly into disaster, if that is what awaited him. Like his fellow adventurers, his fellow nominees for the Gallery of Dishonor, he lacked the ability to restrain himself. He could not curb his appetites.

They all had the same lack: Insull, Kreuger, Ponzi, Stavitsky. Each had lived a youth of drudgery and despair. Samuel Insull remembered life as a dollar-and-a-quarter helper to a London auctioneer, while he was learning an art (to be exploited later in Chicago) of pyramiding millions of dollars into hundreds of millions. Ivar Kreuger, the Swedish Match King, recalled panhandling on the streets of New York as a prelude to bilking investors out of $500,000,000. Italian-born Charles Ponzi was making $15 a week as a stock clerk in Boston while visions of foreign exchange were dancing through his head; those idle fancies, translated into his own particular brand of "reality," were to bring him $15,000,000 in a single year. In France (where pawnshops are a government monopoly) the Russian-born Stavitsky climbed his golden ladder on rungs of phony jewelry and forged bonds in a pawnshop scandal that rocked the country and overthrew the government. Anthony DeAngelis, who hid behind the Fifth Amendment when asked to explain the "disappearance" of nearly 150,000,000 pounds of soy-bean oil allegedly stored in New Jersey tanks, was a hog butcher twenty-five years ago when Coster had already invented the technique of the fictitious inventory. These were men who started with nothing but the lust for adventure and the lure of its golden fruits. The millions they amassed never made them rich, for they were always too poor to stop needing more.

F. Donald Coster could never forget the taste of poverty that had been so bitter in Philip Musica's mouth. He, too, was one of the breed whose hunger could never be appeased. He, too, was a comrade in alms, constantly soliciting fate.

Shakespeare described this company well in the line, "Beggars mounted run their horse to death."

Index